About Demos

Who we are

Demos is the think tank for everyday democracy. We believe everyone should be able to make personal choices in their daily lives that contribute to the common good. Our aim is to put this democratic idea into practice by working with organisations in ways that make them more effective and legitimate.

What we work on

We focus on six areas: public services; science and technology; cities and public space; people and communities; arts and culture; and global security.

Who we work with

Our partners include policy-makers, companies, public service providers and social entrepreneurs. Demos is not linked to any party but we work with politicians across political divides. Our international network – which extends across Eastern Europe, Scandinavia, Australia, Brazil, India and China – provides a global perspective and enables us to work across borders.

How we work

Demos knows the importance of learning from experience. We test and improve our ideas in practice by working with people who can make change happen. Our collaborative approach means that our partners share in the creation and ownership of new ideas.

What we offer

We analyse social and political change, which we connect to innovation and learning in organisations. We help our partners show thought leadership and respond to emerging policy challenges.

How we communicate

As an independent voice, we can create debates that lead to real change. We use the media, public events, workshops and publications to communicate our ideas. All our books can be downloaded free from the Demos website.

www.demos.co.uk

First published in 2007
© Demos
Some rights reserved – see copyright licence for details

ISBN 978 1 84180 180 3
Copy edited by Julie Pickard, London
Typeset by utimestwo, Collingtree, Northants
Printed by IPrint, Leicester

For further information and
subscription details please contact:

Demos
Magdalen House
136 Tooley Street
London SE1 2TU

telephone: 0845 458 5949
email: hello@demos.co.uk
web: www.demos.co.uk

Recruitment 2020

How recruitment is changing and why it matters

Niamh Gallagher
Duncan O'Leary

DEM©S

Contents

Acknowledgements

First, thanks go to Roger Tweedy, Reno Pelekanou and Andre McGarrigle for making this project possible and to John Craig and Sarah Gillinson for their roles in the project early on.

From Demos, thanks to all the interns who helped support the project – Iason Gabriel, Louise Wise, Christopher White, Tom Richardson and Nicholas Carter. Special thanks to Emilie Glazer and Anna Shandro for all their help during the research.

Thanks to Grahame Broadbelt for all his support during the project and to Pete Harrington, Mark Fuller, Simon Parker and Celia Hannon for helping us to sharpen and clarify the final argument.

Finally, thanks to all those who talked with us about their thoughts and experiences during the research.

As ever, all errors and omissions remain our own.

Niamh Gallagher and Duncan O'Leary
April 2007

Executive summary

The research

This report is the result of nine months of Demos research, focused on developing possible futures – or scenarios – for recruitment, and to identify their implications for the industry and for public policy more broadly. *Recruitment 2020* presents the findings and recommendations from our research.

The research process involved over 40 interviews with experts – recruitment agencies, advertisers, employers, interest groups and civil servants; and specialists in diversity, privacy and technology – a futures thinking workshop with industry professionals, and a wide-ranging literature review. Throughout the pamphlet, we adopt the broadest possible definition of the recruitment industry, encompassing everything from outsourcing of temporary and permanent recruitment to advertising and job sites. This represents the most comprehensive and holistic review of the future of recruitment undertaken by any British think tank.

Aims of the study

This report has three aims:

- o   to offer a guide to those operating in the market for recruitment, from employers and recruitment companies to job seekers themselves, to the important trends shaping

    society – and their likely implications
- O   to suggest ways of improving the efficiency and fairness of the market for recruitment companies by giving that market a clear sense of the future
- O   to identify a key set of social challenges which we believe will not be met through the market – and to make recommendations designed to help address those challenges.

Our argument

We argue that the traditional divide between extremely personalised recruitment for highly skilled jobs and relatively standardised recruitment processes for low-skilled jobs looks set to close in the coming years. A combination of new expectations and new opportunities, we suggest, will drive a more personalised approach across the spectrum.

This traditional division is set out in table 1 opposite.

Drivers of change

The new model of recruitment outlined in this pamphlet is the result of a series of drivers of change, identified and explored during the research process. The implications of these drivers, along with a set of tensions they provoke, are explored in depth in part 1 of the report.

A competitive business environment

The recruitment business landscape has changed remarkably over the past decade. The industry has grown rapidly, diversifying its services and making record profits year on year. The war for talent, the growing importance of soft skills, the drive for efficiency and the need for flexibility have all led to an increase in outsourcing and advertising to recruiters and greater efforts to reach candidates through advertising on and offline.

Regulation and legislation

Despite being the 'freest market in Europe', the UK recruitment

Table 1 Two models of recruitment

Highly skilled jobs (highly personalised service)	Low-skilled jobs (more standardised service)
Specific role to be filled	Generic roles to be filled
Certified skills required *plus tacit judgements about suitability*	Certified skills required
Low volume, high cost	High volume, low cost
Identify candidates through networks and peer-to-peer recommendation	Identify candidates through database
Candidate pool from active *and* passive job seekers (people approached about jobs)	Candidate pool from active job seekers only (people looking for jobs)
Candidate interest in pay *plus wider set of factors about role and organisation (progression, company ethic etc)*	Candidate interest in pay
Build relationships with clients and candidates	Functional communication when necessary

industry still faces a set of regulatory and legislative challenges. An unregulated market and the lack of an official, enforceable set of standards bring reputation and standards into question. Important legislation around workplace rights brings issues of compliance and risk management to the fore for recruiters, employers and advertisers.

A changing workforce

Over the coming years, the workforce is set to become far more diverse, reflecting trends towards an ageing population, greater ethnic diversity, increases in immigration and more women taking up positions in paid work. Here, the recruitment industry plays an essential role as intermediary – helping business understand and accept these changes, and encouraging candidates from this 'new' talent pool to enter or re-enter the workforce.

Changing social values

The overlap between life and work – the person and the professional – is growing. Terms and conditions of work, beyond pay – company ethos, the psychological contract, corporate social responsibility (CSR) and ethics – are increasingly important to candidates seeking work. This makes recruitment a more complex process – as recruiters are asked to match *people* with *organisations*, not just skills with vacancies.

Technology

Web 2.0 has become shorthand for a shift in the way the internet is used and understood. It sees the internet as a collaborative tool, where we each have an active role in creating value for one another. Web 2.0 has fundamentally changed recruitment, putting relationships at its very core. Technology too has changed the recruitment *experience*, from the design and distribution of ads to day-on-the-job simulations. But technology has its limits – how much can we rely on it in recruitment?

Combined, the drivers create a serious challenge to the traditional model of recruitment in the UK.

Our recommendations
Beyond the traditional model

We make a series of recommendations to support this process. Employers should:

1   ensure that commissioning processes – whether through human resources (HR) or procurement – focus on value rather than cost
2   align HR, public relations and marketing and be clear about core organisational values.

Recruitment professionals should:

1   track retention to demonstrate impact
2   demand accountable advertising online to demonstrate impact
3   help organisations learn about themselves by overcoming the insider/outsider problem
4   align the recruitment experience with client ethos
5   find ways to connect with the passive job seeker
6   broker and utilise peer-to-peer relationships
7   use Web 2.0 to build personalised relationships online
8   tap into the long tail.

These recommendations are developed in chapter 6.

Markets and social policy

The theme running throughout this pamphlet is both the ingenuity and shortcomings of markets. We argue that many of the likely changes in the market for recruitment will have positive consequences. However, for all their uses, markets often produce imperfect results. They can produce disparities in power which undermine people's ability to shape their own lives. Their outcomes can overlap with social goals, such as more inclusive workplaces, without ever fully achieving them. And markets can be very poor forums for *collective* decisions about the kind of society that we want to live in; the sum of our individual choices often produces outcomes that none of us are comfortable with.

We have identified three social challenges that we consider *beyond the market*, and keeping our focus on recruitment we make recommendations for:

O   *making markets work for people*: through an eBay-style system of self-regulation and peer-to-peer feedback
O   *helping organisations diversify their workforces*: through adding a fifth core goal to sector skills councils' remit – 'to

attract the widest possible pool of talent into the industry
– involving new and different people from all
backgrounds to work and prosper in the sector'

o *securing privacy in the information age*: through advising
young people about potential dangers to their career that
could be caused by this culture clash between high levels
of openness on websites like YouTube.com and the
relatively closed organisational cultures of the corporate
world.

This report is intended to open up a new debate about recruitment in
the UK. Until now, much of the discussion has taken place within the
industry. It is now time for a broader and more ambitious public
debate about recruitment.

Our research demonstrates that recruitment is caught up in some
of the key public policy issues of our time – integration and diversity,
privacy and the regulation of the internet, and competition and
economic success. In this sense the *ability* and *responsibility* of those
in recruitment to influence and bring about change should not be
taken lightly.

Introduction

Every individual . . . neither intends to promote the public interest, nor knows how much he is promoting it . . . he is . . . led by an invisible hand to promote an end which was no part of his intention.

Adam Smith

In 1776 Adam Smith wrote of an 'invisible hand' at work in society.[1] With this metaphor he described the almost mystical ability of the market to meet people's needs. To match what is possible with what is required. Supply with demand.

Sitting at his desk in Kirkcaldy over 200 years ago, the intellectual godfather of capitalism could not have imagined the complexity of today's marketplace.[2] He could not have anticipated the astonishing advances in technology, the ferocious global competition, or the flows of people across continents. Doing business in the twenty-first century has become a difficult proposition.

In the face of this complexity, markets have developed their own responses. New organisations have emerged to help *connect* supply with demand. Where expertise is required, distances are too great, or information is incomplete, intermediaries play a role in solving those problems.

This shift to multi-layered markets has two important implications: first that intermediaries have become hugely important to us.

They mediate many of our personal and professional relationships, providing us with new opportunities, guiding and shaping our choices. Advisers, experts and brokers tell us where to shop, who to do business with – and who to hire.

Our happiness and our wealth can depend on them.

Second, like all markets, those in which intermediaries operate can be either efficient or inefficient. Fair or unfair. Able or unable to operate in the public interest. Where Adam Smith had faith that markets would inevitably serve in the public interest, today we are not so sure. We recognise that their success or failure can be affected by values, incentives, accountability and information.

This pamphlet explores the future of one of the most important intermediaries in our everyday lives: the recruitment industry. At a time when 60 per cent of employees are actively looking for new positions[3] and 85 per cent of organisations report recruitment difficulties,[4] it examines the way in which recruitment connects people's hopes and aspirations with real-life opportunities.

Throughout the pamphlet, we adopt the broadest possible definition of the recruitment industry, encompassing everything from outsourcing of temporary and permanent recruitment to advertising and job sites. We explore the implications of a number of sweeping changes across society, including new legislation, significant advances in technology, changing demographics and shifting social values.

Through our analysis of these trends, we argue that recruitment practices and business models will change immeasurably over the coming years, with implications for:

o business success
o job satisfaction
o equality
o integration
o privacy.

We tell a story of the wide-scale change that we expect to see through the market – and we explore the social challenges that go beyond what the market can deliver alone. In this way, we provide a series of recommendations designed to help both the recruitment industry and wider society prepare for the challenges of the future. In doing so, our aim has been to make this pamphlet relevant not just to policy-makers, but to anyone involved in either seeking or offering a job in the future.

In chapters 1–5 we explore a series of key driving forces which we believe will affect – and *be affected by* – the industry in the coming years. Those driving forces are: a competitive business environment, regulation and legislation, changing demographics, shifting social values and new technology. We conclude each of these chapters by highlighting a series of tensions for the future.

In chapter 6 we describe the implications of these driving forces and make recommendations for the industry itself. We argue that the traditional divide between extremely personalised recruitment for highly skilled jobs and relatively standardised recruitment processes for low-skilled jobs looks set to close in the coming years. A combination of new expectations and new opportunities, we suggest, will drive a more personalised approach across the spectrum.

In chapter 7 we turn to a wider set of social concerns that we believe will not be addressed through the market. We focus on three issues – making markets work for people, helping businesses diversify their workforces and issues around personal privacy – as we make recommendations for government and others to take forward. Finally, we conclude the pamphlet with a summary of our argument and recommendations.

Part 1:
Forces driving change

1. A competitive business environment

'We're not in the business of selling people, we're in the business of selling information', remarked one of our interviewees. His comment illustrated something that helps to explain the remarkable growth of the recruitment industry over the last decade: in the modern economy knowledge *is* power.

As the British economy shifts away from the standardised jobs and processes of the industrial revolution towards 'knowledge economy' and service sector jobs (see figure 1) business success depends in large part on human factors. The number of 'standardised' roles is shrinking – organisations from all sectors increasingly want *particular* people to fill *particular* roles.

This chapter explores this trend further and relates it to the growth, shape and activity within the recruitment market. It charts the growth of the industry over the last decade and argues that this growth is the product of:

o   the 'war for talent' between organisations across the economy
o   the increasing importance of soft skills – and therefore the emphasis on tacit decisions involved in recruiting for attitudes and behaviours and competencies
o   the growth in outsourcing as a means to access expertise and flexible-just-in-time services.

Figure 1 The shift to knowledge and service sector jobs to 2020

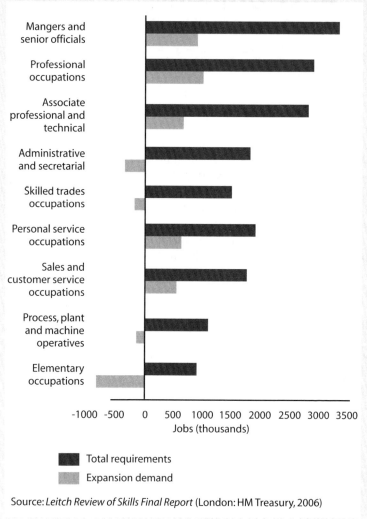

Source: *Leitch Review of Skills Final Report* (London: HM Treasury, 2006)

The 'war for talent'

Finding the right people matters. And it matters whether you own a restaurant or an investment bank. The skills of the chef or the waiter differ from those of the city trader, but the unifying feature is that both businesses compete on the combined abilities of their employees.

Though the benefits of the 'intangible' assets brought by people can be hard to quantify, the evidence suggests that they are growing steadily. Accenture calculates that 'intangibles' accounted for 20 per cent of the value of the top 500 companies in the US in 1980, compared with around 70 per cent in 2006.[5] The consultants McKinsey & Company – whose own organisational training budget stands at £100 million[6] – describe this as 'the war for talent'. 'All that matters is talent. Talent wins,' they insist.[7]

'Soft skills' and innovation

Beyond finding highly qualified employees, however, organisations across sectors are becoming more precise about a further set of skills and capacities that they are looking for.

As companies seek to find ways to compete in highly competitive markets, many are becoming much more discerning about *which* skills they are looking for in potential employees. While both academic and vocational qualifications remain in high demand, a glance at where companies identify skills shortages, as shown in figure 2, indicates the increasing importance of a broader set of personal capacities.[8] Qualifications are necessary but not sufficient in the modern workplace.

In a growing service economy, interpersonal skills and initiative are valued as companies seek to enhance customer service. Employees must help create enjoyable *experiences* as well as high-quality food, or a comfortable stay in a hotel. And with an emphasis on innovation across the economy, creativity is becoming seen as an important quality now – and a non-negotiable for the future. Demos research published in 2006 found that human resources (HR) directors in FTSE 250 companies ranked 'creativity and innovation' as the most

Figure 2 Skills gaps and skills shortage vacancies (2004)

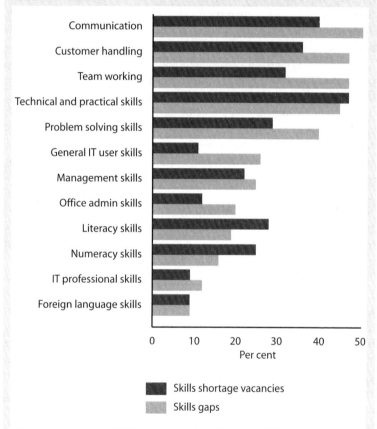

Source: Learning and Skills Council, *National Employer Skills Survey* (London: LSC, 2004)

important skills for graduates in ten years' time – above numeracy, literacy and IT skills.[9]

As companies become clearer about their own comparative advantages – and more precise about what that means for who they want to employ – recruitment becomes both an important and a difficult process. Many of the employers that we spoke to during this research identified recruiting on the basis of attitudes and behaviours as an important trend for the future. This reflects research from the United States suggesting that while employers used to appoint candidates on the basis of 90 per cent experience and 10 per cent attitude, that situation has now changed to around 40 per cent on attitude and a series of 'soft skills'.[10]

Employees with high skills are required, but subjective, tacit judgements about people's personal qualities and approach to work are needed, in order to identify candidates with the right blend of skills, behaviours and aspirations. Organisations are looking not just for employees with track records of success – but also evidence that *the way that person works* will fit with the ethos of their organisation. Are they a team player? What approach – as well as which qualities – will they bring with them?

> *We don't just want to know that a manager doubled turnover. We want to know how they did that. Does their personal style fit with the ethos and values here?*
>
> Interviewee, employer

Outsourcing

And if market signals tell us anything, it is that businesses see recruitment companies as an important ally in negotiating this complex terrain. According to the Chartered Institute of Personnel and Development (CIPD), 83 per cent of organisations used recruitment organisations in 2004, for a variety of reasons ranging from speed to skills shortages.[11]

This popularity reflects a trend in recent years for organisations to examine all of their own functions – and to question which of those functions could be performed more efficiently and effectively by another organisation. One study in 2004 found that over 90 per cent of organisations surveyed had outsourced at least one element of activity to another organisation. Further, nearly a fifth had outsourced work done by their own employees in the past.[12]

More and more companies are off-shoring back office functions to Asian countries, where they can be done for half the price, and in a different time zone – often allowing companies to operate 24 hours a day. Further, companies are finding that outsourcing elements of their business adds flexibility to their business models. Organisations are able to buy in services without the risk of taking on greater numbers of staff themselves. These, therefore, help them respond to new opportunities quickly, through accessing just-in-time services without tying their hands for the future.

The growth and shape of the industry

For these core reasons – the importance of talent, the increasing precision in recruitment, the drive for efficiency and the option of flexibility – recruiting has become a growth industry over the last decade, with turnover for the industry rising from less than £10 billion to nearly £25 billion in less than a decade, as shown in figure 3.[13] The bulk of this revenue (around four-fifths) comes from recruitment for temporary positions, with the remainder coming from permanent placements.

However, in spite of this remarkable growth over the last ten years profit margins have begun to be reigned in. The volume of placements has increased at a higher rate than turnover in 2005 indicating that more work is being done, for less money than in the past. This is explainable by a combination of ferocious competition (discussed in the next chapter), but also by the emergence of vendor management, or recruitment process outsourcing (RPO) – a business model designed to help companies make savings through improving the commissioning process itself. Companies operating in this space between contractors and contractees claim significant savings for their clients.

Figure 3 Overall turnover of recruitment companies to 2005

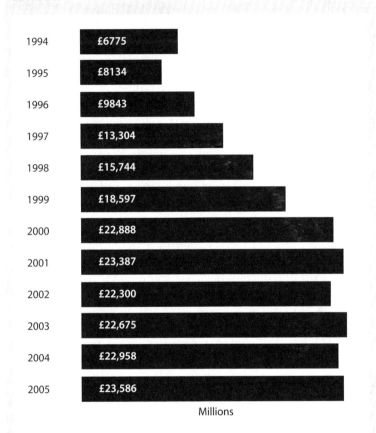

1994	£6775
1995	£8134
1996	£9843
1997	£13,304
1998	£15,744
1999	£18,597
2000	£22,888
2001	£23,387
2002	£22,300
2003	£22,675
2004	£22,958
2005	£23,586

Millions

Source: REC and Ernst and Young, *Annual Industry Turnover and Key Volumes Survey 2005/2006* (2006)

Recruitment advertising

Alongside the long-term growth in both temporary and permanent recruitment, there has been an explosion in online advertising. A generation ago the print media's dominance in advertising looked unchallengeable but the emergence of the internet, the rise of job sites, the low cost and speed of advertising online, and companies' use of their own websites has challenged that position.

In 2006 recruitment advertising in print generated a total of £1.168 billion in revenues (down 13 per cent for the year) with online advertising worth £200.5 million (up 27 per cent).[14] In a world in which 62 per cent of all UK adults are online, 50 per cent of internet users go online each day and there are 12 million online job seekers in UK, the web is an increasingly important way of connecting with potential employees.[15]

As a result of this:

O   65 per cent of FTSE 100 companies use the internet to recruit candidates.[16]

O   78 per cent of recruitment companies advertise job vacancies online.[17]

O   UK job sites currently receive around 40 million visits per month.[18]

O   Monster.co.uk alone has over two million CVs on its website.[19]

The internet is also blurring the old, neat divisions between advertisers and recruiters. Websites are taking on some traditional recruitment functions, particularly where employers are looking to fill low-skilled jobs at minimum cost, while both employers and recruitment companies are investing in their online capability as a way of connecting directly with potential applicants.

Tensions for the future

As the markets for advertising and outsourcing mature, there are several key questions, or tensions, for the future.

Recruitment vs retention

In a competitive economy and a public sector where spending is being reigned in, organisations are beginning to realise that they can no longer be satisfied with short-term solutions. Recruiting staff only for them to leave again shortly afterwards can be an expensive business – and organisations are turning their attention to successful retention in order to guard against that expense.

Similarly, the public sector has been criticised for spending vast swathes of money on agency workers[20] – it was estimated in 2006 that the NHS spends £1 billion a year on agency staff[21] – rather than simply taking on permanent staff for a much reduced overall cost. This represents a challenge to organisations across sectors to think more strategically about recruitment – focusing less on short-term cost and more on long-term value for money.

Though difficult to calculate precisely, a recent CIPD survey estimated that the average turnover cost per employee is £8200, rising to £12,000 for senior managers or directors.[22] These figures emphasise the value of identifying staff retention as a strategic priority.

One of the key issues raised in our interviews with both employers and recruiters was a failure by HR departments to keep track of staff, in order to identify whether how they were recruited (direct vs via agency) had an impact on how long they stayed. Increasingly, recruitment agencies may no longer be judged on the number of candidates they place in jobs, but on the number of candidates that remain in those same jobs a year later.

One-off savings vs long-term efficiency

Control of recruitment in large organisations is often a tug-of-war between HR and procurement departments. Priorities differ profoundly depending on who gains control – HR can often focus on long-term investment and development, while procurement is concerned with keeping costs to a minimum. As the figures above demonstrate, costs should not outweigh value in recruitment – more metrics and tighter evaluation procedures are required if long-term efficiency is the aim.

Some would point to RPOs as a route to long-term efficiency. But while RPOs can lay claim on significant savings, removing any slack in the market and driving margins down as low as possible, this process has a natural limit: the point at which companies can no longer make a profit at all. Similarly, in the public sector, where local authorities and government departments are in the process of merging back-room functions (and therefore recruitment) as a result of the Gershon review on efficiency, these measures represent one-off savings. Merging two departments cannot happen more than once.

At this point, when the market has corrected itself (or the public sector has completed the Gershon changes), the need remains to find systematic ways to improve efficiency, beyond eliminating slack in the system, in the long term.

Traditional vs new models for advertising

As advertising platforms diversify a key challenge for organisations will be to integrate different communications channels as part of a coherent overall strategy. As the old defaults are replaced by a plethora of new options it will be necessary to identify the added value of different platforms. Strategists will need to recognise the ways that different platforms do different things – from heightening brand visibility to reaching different parts of an ever-diversifying workforce.Where and how organisations in the public and private sectors advertise has important implications for who their message reaches and how they are perceived. Linked to the shift to advertising online is the rise of 'accountable advertising', which we discuss in chapter 6.

2. Regulation and legislation

Try starting a business in two different countries and it is likely that your enterprise will be up and running in one of those countries days – possibly weeks – before the other. In Spain it takes, on average, 47 days to set up a business compared with a figure of just two days in Australia.[23] This reflects an important point: that governments create and set the terms of markets, and can prioritise different objectives – from leanness and efficiency to trust, security and protection for those operating within them.

This chapter explores the impact of legislation and regulation on the recruitment industry in Britain. It argues that:

○ part of the explanation for the large number of firms in the recruitment market lies in the low barriers to entry for those wishing to enter the market

○ this level of choice and ease of entry means that, for potential clients of the industry, information is at a premium to ensure that they are able to choose firms that deliver value for money

○ legislation providing rights in the workplace for all employees has been important in addressing asymmetries of power between employees and employers – but also that a side-effect has been to make recruitment more risk-laden.

An open market

In the market for recruitment companies, the government has adopted the principle that maximum competition is the most likely route to ensure value for money for clients of the industry – and that low barriers to entry are the best way of generating that competition. One clear consequence of this is the existence of a high number of small businesses in the industry (see figure 4). With the market at its most open, new enterprises can start as quickly as old ones wither away.

That [an open market] must account for the explosion of companies over the last ten years – the low barriers to entry lead to many more people trying their luck.

Interviewee, analyst

The relative openness of the market also perhaps explains the way in which the extremely rapid growth that the recruitment industry witnessed in the late 1990s appears now to have given way to a period of sustained but steady long-term growth. The levelling off of growth in the industry – described in the last chapter – suggests that the market is reaching a level of saturation or equilibrium; though new companies continue to emerge, replacing those that are least successful, the total spend in the market seems to be levelling off.

Like many markets with high levels of choice for customers and low barriers to entry for companies, information is at a premium for clients of the industry looking to contract out elements of recruitment. Choice and competition are useful tools, but only when a level of information is available to ensure that choices are not arbitrary, and that positive feedback loops are established that reward excellent service with more business in the future.

With this in mind, those concerned with the overall health of the market (and therefore reputation of the industry) have taken steps to provide clearer information about those companies offering services.

Figure 4 Number of enterprises engaged in recruitment and provision of personnel by employee sizeband (2004)

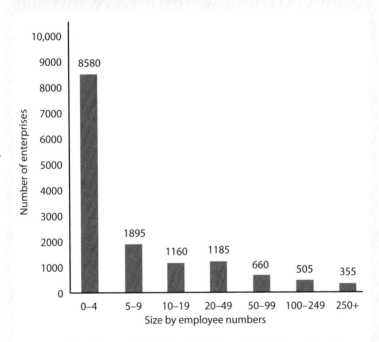

Source: Office of National Statistics, *UK Business: Activity, size and location* (2004)

Information schemes

As part of the drive to provide clearer information in the market there are a number of accreditation schemes, certifying both business and ethical credentials. These include:

○ *a code of practice*: in the form of nine statements of principle supported by specific promises, accompanied by an auditing scheme which allows agencies to prove that they are living up to their commitment to the code of practice

O   *a diversity pledge*: through which agencies commit to going beyond the requirements of the law in delivering diversity excellence

O   *a quality mark for education agencies*: to illustrate credentials to work in that sector.[24]

Gangmasters legislation

One area where government does play an active role is through the Gangmasters Licensing Authority (GLA). The GLA was established through a private members' bill in parliament following the deaths of 21 Chinese cockle pickers in Morecombe Bay in February 2004.

This legislation reflected a decision to prioritise safety and a set of moral concerns over the dynamism and profitability of the market. As with the introduction of the minimum wage, an act of law helped society take a collective decision about the kind of practices that are acceptable in a market. The bill also illustrates a wider principle: where markets can create asymmetries of power between organisations and individuals – leaving employees vulnerable to exploitation – governments can and should step in to ensure that those individuals are protected.

Workplace rights

Another area where government has made similar decisions to intervene in markets in order to protect the wellbeing and life chances of individuals has been in legislation introducing rights in the workplace. Box 1 identifies the key areas of legislation in this area – illustrating the way in which individuals have steadily gained more protection in the workplace over the last few decades.

The effects of this legislation – including the recent Age Discrimination Act – are widely thought to have been positive in protecting people from prejudice in the workplace and the wider labour market. One side-effect for organisations, however, has been that the process of recruitment has become a riskier business, with more legislation to comply with.

I think this [the age legislation] can only be a good thing – for one thing it encourages employers to look at people skills and abilities rather than make lazy assumptions about 'experience' or 'youthfulness'.

Interviewee, recruiter

Box 1 Legislation introducing rights in the workplace[25]

The Equal Pay Act (1970) established the principle of assuring individuals of either gender the same pay and benefits for equivalent work.

The Sex Discrimination Act (1975) outlawed direct discrimination on the basis of gender in employment, education, advertising or the provision of housing, goods, services or facilities.

The Race Relations Act (1976) provided legal remedies against indirect discrimination.

The Disability Discrimination Act (1995) addressed disability discrimination in employment and the provision of services and attempted to establish a level playing field for disabled people in employment and the provision of goods and services.

The Race Relations Amendment Act (2000) carried with it a duty on the public sector to promote racial equality.

The Employment Equality Regulations (2003) introduced by the EU brought religion and belief, sexual orientation and age within the scope of employment discrimination law.

Age Discrimination Act (2006) aimed to ensure that a person of any age has an equal chance of employment, training and promotion.

Advice and guidance

These increasing levels of complexity perhaps help explain the way in which an outpouring of advice regarding 'best practice' has taken place, to accompany various elements of legislation. As Britain's working population has diversified – from more women in the workforce to greater ethnic diversity – organisations have been asked to become more sensitive to hidden biases in procedures.

It's [recent legislation] certainly led to a lot of training – we've been running lots of workshops with key clients to bring them up to speed with the changes.

Interviewee, recruiter

Perhaps in response to the legislation, and perhaps in response to their own desire not to miss out on the chance to employ people from all sections of the population, organisations themselves have invested greater amounts of money in training their staff in this area. The CIPD reports that:

O in 2003, 54 per cent of organisations had equal opportunities training for interviewing
O in 2004, 67 per cent had this training
O in 2005, 69 per cent had this training.[26]

These trends towards an open market for recruitment companies and increased workplace protection raise some interesting questions for the future.

Tensions

Dynamism of the free market vs trust and wider social goals of a regulated one

Since Adam Smith wrote *The Wealth of Nations* over two centuries ago,[27] economists, philosophers, politicians and people in business have argued about the merits and demerits of the free market. A key question for the future is how to maintain dynamism while injecting trust and fairness into markets.

A key element here is ensuring that markets have a sense of the future – future rewards for excellence and future consequences for poor performance. Both regulation and information-rich markets can provide this, creating an incentive for the companies to deliver value when contracts have been agreed and signed off.

The danger of removing the person from the employee, rather than understanding them

In the (much needed) attempts to root out intentional and unintentional prejudice from recruitment procedures, guidance needs to avoid attempting to remove the person altogether from the interviewee. As we saw in the last chapter, organisations increasingly *look to make* decisions based on behaviours, personality types and attitudes – and if guidance is unable to engage with this then it risks becoming irrelevant.

In this context, there is a clear tension with the employers' priorities and guidance which suggests that 'employers should avoid making references part of the selection process', as the Commission for Racial Equality (CRE) does, or suggesting that telephone interviewing can be useful as it can help interviewers focus directly on skills and experiences, as does some of the guidance from the Equal Opportunities Commission.[28]

Unrealistic guidance is hardly the main problem we face as a society, particularly when set against the discrimination suffered by people over the years. However, the danger is that guidance that does not reflect the realities of the modern workplace will carry no credibility with employers.

Diversity on interview panels themselves and training in this area are the best ways of actually understanding people, rather than ignoring their personal characteristics.

3. A changing workforce

In 1989 the DIY retailer B&Q opened an outlet in Macclesfield. The new store enjoyed low turnover of staff, low levels of absenteeism, high profits and soon established a positive image in the local community. It was also staffed entirely by over 50s. The success of this organisational experiment pushed the company to develop its over-50s recruitment policy, and it now boasts that of a total staff of 37,000, 22 per cent are over 50.

This story is both illuminating and unusual – illuminating because it indicates one of a number of important ways in which the workforce is changing in the UK, but unusual because many organisations have been far slower than B&Q to respond to shifting demographics.

This chapter explores the implications of those changing demographics in relation to recruitment. It argues that:

O   the declining number of white, able-bodied men under 45
    in the workforce in the coming years will lead to
    employers having to diversify their workforces, to some
    extent at least
O   the position of a number of social groups in society
    cannot be explained through factors like educational
    achievement or even social class.

Changing demographics

By 2010, only 20 per cent of the UK's full-time workforce will comprise white, able-bodied men under 45.[29] Over the coming years, the workforce is set to become far more diverse, reflecting trends towards an ageing population, greater ethnic diversity and more women taking up positions in paid work.

Yet research also indicates that there is much more to be done if people from all backgrounds, ages and family circumstances are to participate successfully in work in the future. The Government's Equalities Review identified a host of persistent 'employment penalties' (see box 2) suggesting that social factors rather than personal choice still dictate many people's career progression. This is demonstrated in figure 5.

Box 2 The employment penalty[30]

An employment penalty is a measure of the disadvantage that individuals or groups face in the labour market.

For instance, when we say that the employment penalty for disabled people is 29 per cent, this means that disabled people are 29 percentage points less likely to be in work than non-disabled people with otherwise similar characteristics, such as age and ethnicity, the level of educational qualifications and family composition.

The presence of this penalty suggests that disability really does reduce people's job chances, but it is not clear from this analysis alone what causes the problem – whether disabled people are unable to work, whether they genuinely prefer not to work, or whether employers discriminate against them.

The employment penalty is therefore different from – and in most cases smaller than – the overall gap in employment rates. It is of course important to be aware of this overall gap, since the fact that part of it is attributable to factors such as different educational qualification rates does not make it any less real.

Figure 5 Employment penalties in the early 2000s (percentage points)

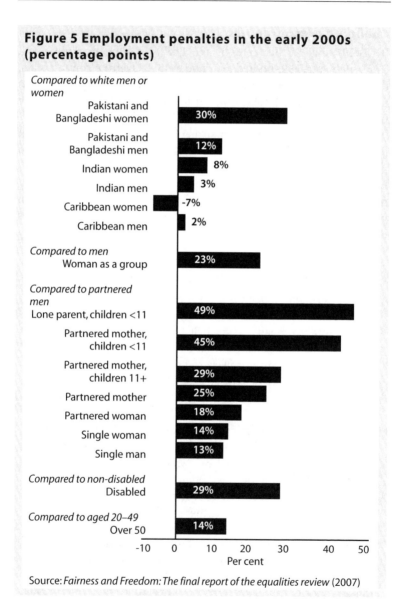

Source: *Fairness and Freedom: The final report of the equalities review* (2007)

As the findings from the review indicated, making sure that equality of opportunity means something in practice requires far more than the freedom to apply for a job – it relates to our everyday perceptions and experiences as well as to formal rights and responsibilities. If someone *feels* discouraged from applying for a role in a particular organisation or industry because of the culture of that organisation or industry then that matters. Because genuine equality must take account of real-world experiences as well as a set of theoretical notions.

This position is fast becoming accepted by those across the political spectrum. As David Cameron argued recently:

> *The fact is that it's not enough just to open the door to ethnic minorities. If people look in and see an all-white room they are less likely to hang around. An unlocked door is not the same as a genuine invitation to come in.*[31]

These issues represent an important set of future challenges for organisations and recruitment companies looking to fill vacancies – and for any government interested in creating a society in which people determine their own life chances.

> *You can get your policy right and your brochure in place, but it's the culture that really matters. Culture and reputation – they're what people make judgements on.*
>
> Interviewee, employer

An ageing population

One of the most obvious and predictable shifts in the nature of the workforce in the coming years is that it will age. The combination of declining birth rates and greater longevity means that by 2030 the number of people aged 50 and over will have reached 46 per cent of the total UK population, rising from 33 per cent in 2002.[32]

In simple terms, this suggests that employers will need to attract and retain greater numbers of older staff than in the past, as figure 6

Figure 6 Demographic change in the workforce

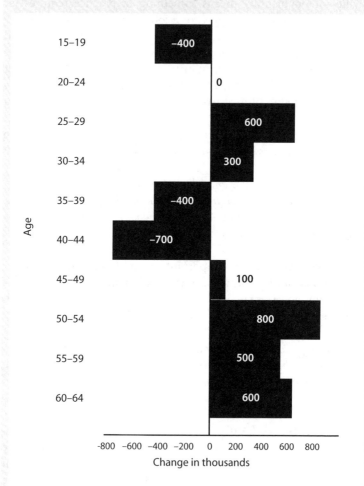

Source: *Leitch Review of Skills Final Report* (London: HM Treasury, 2006)

demonstrates. To add to this, though, there is a set of trends that are likely to see members of that generation themselves more amenable to the idea of working beyond the traditional retirement age. Changes to the pensions system are likely to make a longer working life a necessity for many people, while there is evidence to suggest that the 'baby boomer' generation is likely to be less inclined to give up work than its predecessors.[33]

> *The pensions crisis is an opportunity for us in many ways – we're going to need that generation to fill jobs.*
>
> Interviewee, recruiter

Ethnic diversity

As the UK's population ages, it seems likely that migration will be required to fill the gap left by people who are either scaling down their working hours or retiring altogether. The government's own predictions suggest that between now and 2020 net migration will account for more than 40 per cent of growth in the working-age population.[34] The effect of this is that by 2020 8 per cent of the workforce will be from an ethnic minority (compared with around 6 per cent today).[35]

However, within the 'ethnic minority population' there are wide variations in levels of educational achievement and success within the labour market, which make it difficult to talk in general terms.

Among those born in this country, people from Indian and Chinese backgrounds are likely to outperform those with Pakistani, Bangladeshi and Caribbean heritage[36] in both education and employment. And, as figure 7 indicates, the picture where immigration is concerned becomes incredibly complex.

All this combines to make 'diversity' an important matter in both economic and social terms, but also a hugely complex one. This raises two issues: first, that organisations may become more 'diverse', while some groups are left behind. And second, that public policy (and language) must find ways of reflecting the huge levels of differentiation within the 'ethnic minority' population.

Figure 7 Participation of migrants in the labour market

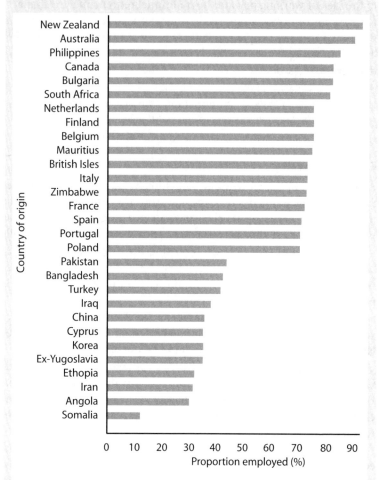

Source: S Kyambi, *Beyond Black and White: Mapping new immigrant communities* (London: ippr, 2005)

There's a lot of woolly thinking around terms like 'diversity' and 'ethnic minorities'. There's such variation between these communities that they [the terms] can sometimes be close to meaningless.

Interviewee, employer

Women in the workforce

Another key change is the continuing trend for more women to enter the workforce. In the UK the numbers of women in work has risen from 59 per cent in 1980 to 70 per cent today.[37] Now, the numbers of men and women at work are almost equal, with men performing 12.8 million jobs and women 12.7 million, though almost half of these are part time. And casting forward, the evidence available suggests that by 2020 women will account for 80 per cent of workforce growth.

But men and women still follow very different career paths. Almost a quarter of women in work do administrative or secretarial work, while men are more likely to be managers, senior officials or work in skilled trades.[38] In part, this funnelling of women into certain roles and industries can be explained by the role of women as primary carers at home. *The Other Glass Ceiling* published by Demos in 2006 showed that women still shoulder a disproportionate amount of the burden in the home – looking after children, managing the household and maintaining social networks – whether or not they are in paid work.[39] And women who do work often choose jobs that offer flexibility – for example they are care assistants, check-out managers or domestics.

The recent Equalities Review placed mothers as one of the top three groups facing 'large and persistent unemployment', showing that mothers (with partners) are 40 per cent less likely to be in work than their male counterparts.[40] Those women who work continue to be paid less than men – the UK boasts the highest gender pay gap in Europe, despite having the third highest female employment rate.[41] Combined with the high cost of childcare this provides adequate disincentive for women to enter or return to work.

Key tensions

Traditional vs future talent pool

The extent of the demographic changes in the coming years will mean that organisations will need to find new and better ways of widening the social groups that they recruit from – whether that applies to attracting candidates from different ethnic backgrounds, or finding ways to connect with working mothers or baby boomers.

As we discuss below, the extent to which these changes create a generic 'business case' for diversity is questionable – businesses may still find some groups easier to reach than others – but the need to connect with a *more* diverse range of potential candidates looks clear.

The 'business case' for diversity vs the statistics

The demographic trends indicate that organisations in all sectors are likely to see their workforces diversify to some extent in the coming years. The effects of population changes and new legislation suggest that this will happen in part through the market and in part because of new rules designed to stamp out prejudice and discrimination.

However, the painfully slow rate of progress in this area suggests that this combination of market forces and prohibitive legislation will not on their own lead to much more than incremental change in the workforces of many organisations and industries. 'Promoting diversity', something that surely means more than 'eliminating discrimination', suggests something more positive than this: the leader of the Conservative party has described this as moving *beyond the unlocked door to the genuine invitation to come in.*

A key question (which we return to in more detail in chapter 7) is whether *individual organisations* will have the time, finance and motivation to extend this invitation to all communities. In short, is there really a 'business case for diversity', as is often argued? Will the market create the kind of opportunity and integration that most people in society regard as important?

Macroeconomic vs social analysis of immigration

Despite economic success, immigration remains a contested and emotive political subject. A recent survey showed that only 5 per cent of the public think that immigration laws should be relaxed or abolished, while 74 per cent believe there are too many immigrants in the UK. Only 18 per cent disagree with this claim.[42] These statistics show the social tensions that remain around immigration, reflecting two key factors:

○ The costs and benefits of immigration are unevenly distributed – the highly educated are far less likely to compete with new arrivals for benefits, housing or a job.

○ Immigration is a *social* as well as an economic phenomenon – migration affects not just the labour market but also the social make-up of communities.

The implication of this is that macroeconomic analysis of the overall benefits of immigration[43] does not guarantee positive attitudes towards more open borders in the coming years. Rather, strategies will need to be found which reflect people's economic and social concerns if the talent pool from abroad is not to dry up.

4. Changing social values

'Better work, better life' promises the strap line of Adecco, a leading recruitment company in the UK. 'We seek those motivated to make change and know that as partners we can help them to shape and achieve their personal and professional goals' continues the blurb on the company's website.[44]

In some senses this fusion of the personal and the professional is nothing new. Confucius, the ancient Chinese philosopher, famously advised, 'Choose a job you love, and you will never have to work a day in your life'. Karl Marx constructed a whole political philosophy around work and identity; and for years businesses have put together narratives about the defining characteristics of 'our people'. Work and life have never been entirely separable.

This chapter explores how social values are shifting and what that means for recruitment in the future. It argues that:

O rising prosperity and a tight labour market means that people can be more discerning about whom they work for – and on what terms

O this means that company values, branding and reputation matter more and more in attracting the best candidates

O recruitment therefore becomes, more and more, about matching *people* with *organisations* – as well as just skills with vacancies

O   more powerful, highly qualified candidates are more likely
    to be able to assert these values and expectations in
    practice.

In some ways the language used by Adecco and its competitors is
extremely telling. The promise not just to improve someone's work
but to improve their *life* reflects a subtle shift in many people's
priorities, with consequences for their expectations of work.

Michael Moynagh, director of the ESRC-funded 'Tomorrow Project',
identifies five areas in which work is playing an increasingly important
role in our personal identities. He suggests that it provides us with:

O   *a structure*: a framework for thinking about life ('this is
    what next week will involve')
O   *a source of income*: to sustain the rest of life
O   *social status*: even a poorly regarded job can seem better
    than being unemployed
O   *companionship*: work colleagues may not always be
    friends, but they do provide company
O   *an opportunity for fulfilment*: at least in some cases.[45]

Adecco's pitch – and the political scramble to take ownership of
'happiness' – suggests that some of these more intangible aspects of
life are becoming increasingly important for both business success
and social policy.

This is perhaps a reflection of a combination of trends towards a
tight labour market and higher living standards (see figures 8 and 9),
which allows many people to bring a whole new set of conditions and
criteria to the decisions that we make. As we become wealthier, we can
afford the luxury of expecting more from work – and many of us
want not just an income but also a quality of life.

In broad terms, organisations are finding ways to adapt their offer
to meet the priorities of potential employees in three key areas:

O   terms and conditions beyond pay
O   intangibles, like company ethos
O   ethics and corporate social responsibility.

Figure 8 Employment rates: UK 16+ unemployment rates (seasonally adjusted)

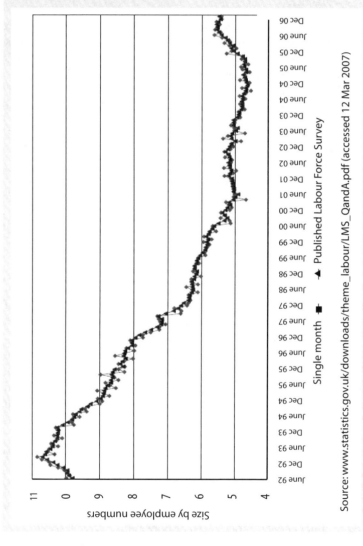

Source: www.statistics.gov.uk/downloads/theme_labour/LMS_QandA.pdf (accessed 12 Mar 2007)

Figure 9 Changes in average real incomes since 1996

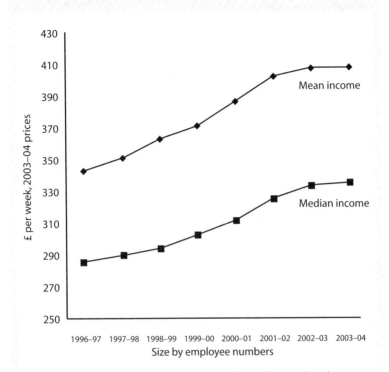

Source: M Brewer et al, *Living Standards, Inequality and Poverty* (London: Institute for Fiscal Studies, 2005)

Terms and conditions

One clear implication of the drive for more personalised or responsive relationships is that the organisational incentives and working arrangements look set to diversify further over the next decade.

Figure 10 Reasons for leaving previous job (2005)

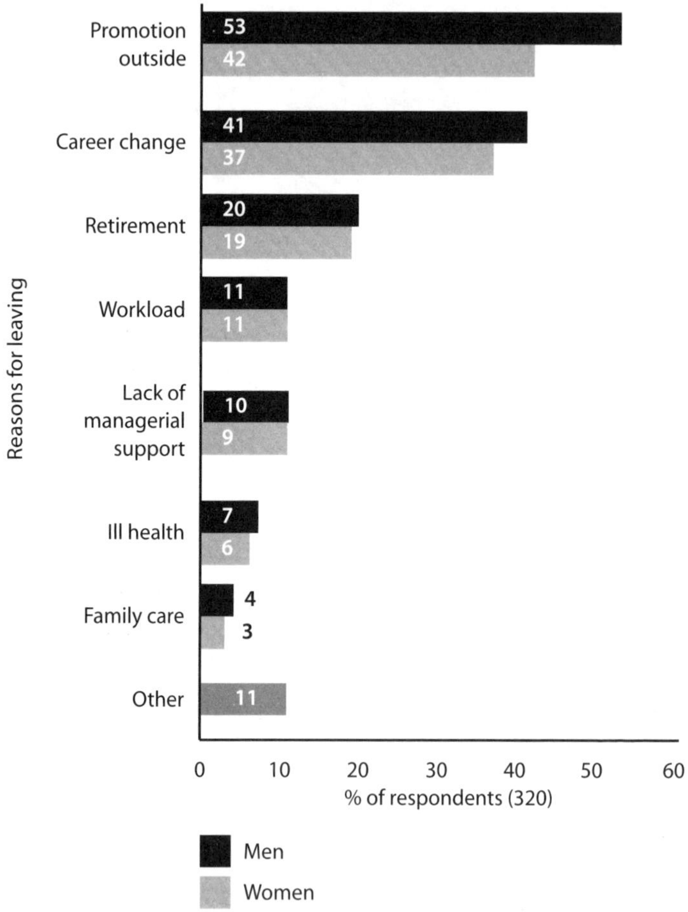

Source: Chartered Institute for Personnel Development, *Recruitment, Retention and Turnover*, 2006 survey

Flexible working is the example cited most often here. The combination of a changing workforce, our wider expectations of work and a deeper set of questions about families and care[46] all suggest that the trend towards more opportunities to work flexibly looks set to continue. Fully 84 per cent of women and 82 per cent of men in full-time jobs would like to spend more time with their family, compared with figures of 75 per cent and 70 per cent, respectively, in 1989.[47] And over 37 per cent of people would like to work fewer hours even if this meant earning less and of those 42 per cent were aged 16–24.[48]

Employers are finding themselves having to respond to new legislation as well as to the demands of their own employees. Flexible working, or course, is not for everyone – and can reduce opportunities for the social contact and camaraderie described in the work of the Tomorrow Project – but the emphasis on making that option available looks set to continue.

Access to *education and training* is another area where there is evidence that some employees, at least, are becoming more demanding of the deals that they strike with employers. While the paternalistic relationships of the past may be withering away, the deal with organisations – for individuals in a position of strength at least – seems to be enhanced *employability* rather than guaranteed employment. As *The Economist* commented in 2006, many employees 'do expect their employer to help them keep their skills up to date . . . clearly the best way for companies to win the talent wars is to turn themselves into learning organisations'.[49]

And linked to access to education and training is the importance of *progression* (see figure 10). In the short run, organisations can provide reward schemes and a positive atmosphere, but a number of recent surveys have shown that promotion and moving up the career ladder are the most important factors when searching for a job.[50]

Company ethos (the psychological contract)

Beyond the formal terms, conditions and incentives on offer in modern organisations, there is a body of research which identifies the importance of the 'psychological contract' between employers and employees.

While this sounds relatively abstract, it is something that most people will recognise: how it *feels* to work somewhere matters. The Chartered Institute for Personnel Development describes the psychological contract as 'the reality of the situation as perceived by the parties, [which] may be more influential than the formal contract in affecting how employees behave from day to day. It is the psychological contract that effectively tells employees what they are required to do in order to meet their side of the bargain, and what they can expect from their job.'[51]

This contract is both challenging and important for organisations seeking to recruit, retain and motivate the best staff: challenging because the contract may be perceived, or framed,[52] in entirely different ways by managers and those working for them in organisations. And important, because of the convergence of HR policy, company branding and new technology, which allows employee dissatisfaction to travel a long way, very quickly, through online sites and networks.[53]

Vault.com is perhaps the clearest manifestation of this. The site invites employees to fill out a survey on their employer, answering questions which range from salary and interview questions to 'general business outlook' – anything from company ethos to office gossip. Vault.com features surveys from over 66,000 employees of 5778 companies. And although it's not Vault's primary aim, it does more than provide insider advice for job seekers.[54]

Vault's influence demands accountability from companies, by creating a space where their rhetoric is tested in reality. Advocating work–life balance in the media is no good if your employees claim to work 16-hour days, and launching a glossy CSR brochure won't wash if people know that office practices discourage responsible behaviour.

Companies lose money when they break formal contracts; they risk losing staff, reputation and pulling power when they break the psychological contract.

Ethics and corporate social responsibility

Closely linked to how it feels to work for an organisation is how it is perceived in – and relates to – the wider world. While many of us want to work for an organisation that promotes our own wellbeing, we also increasingly expect organisations to act in ethical ways where broader social issues are concerned. According to Business in the Community, 88 per cent of British employees believe that it is important that the organisation they work for is committed to living its values,[55] while 47 per cent of job seekers say they are more likely to join a company that addresses social issues.[56]

The trend is clearest among graduates, who are young, powerful and can often afford to worry about more than their basic rate of pay. As figure 11 indicates, the survey evidence shows a clear correlation between the attractiveness of an employer and perceptions as to how seriously that organisation takes its responsibility to society.

And when individuals find themselves inside organisations, they also report higher levels of commitment towards companies that they can identify with. Figure 12 shows findings from MORI research in this area.

Where employees are able to bring these kinds of priorities to decisions about where to work, the process of recruitment becomes more complex. Processes cannot simply be about matching skills with job vacancies, but rather about matching *people* with *companies* – increasing the importance of branding, image and tacit judgements about which candidates will be best suited to which organisations. This suggests that there will be increasing value in investing in relationships with clients and job seekers to fully understand the needs of both.

Key tensions
Reported values vs actual behaviour

Though there are clearly discernible shifts in preferences of people across society when it comes to work, there is always a danger of mistaking what people say drives their decision-making for what

Figure 11 Graduate values

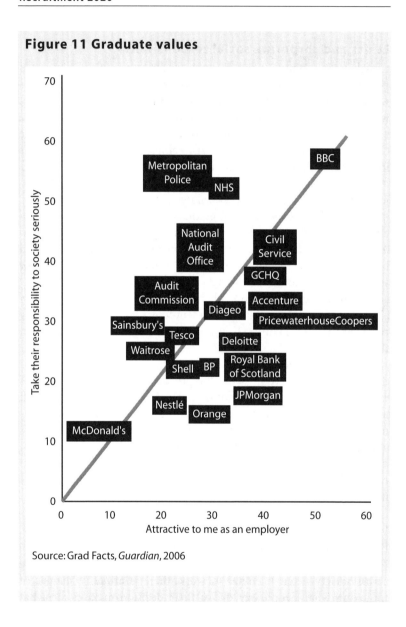

Source: Grad Facts, *Guardian*, 2006

Figure 12 Corporate social responsibility and retention

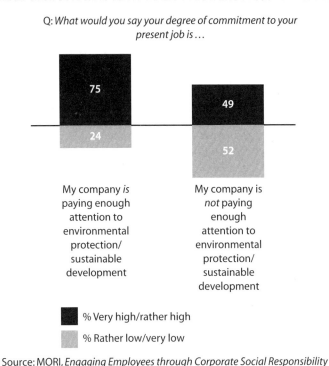

Q: *What would you say your degree of commitment to your present job is …*

My company *is* paying enough attention to environmental protection/ sustainable development

My company is *not* paying enough attention to environmental protection/ sustainable development

■ % Very high/rather high

░ % Rather low/very low

Source: MORI, *Engaging Employees through Corporate Social Responsibility* (London: MORI, 2006)

actually influences behaviour in practice. We know, for example, that 30 per cent of consumers claim to care about companies' environmental and social track records, yet only 3 per cent channel these beliefs into their purchasing preferences.[57] Linked to this is an ongoing debate about the 'portfolio career' – the suggestion that people are becoming more discerning about whom they work for and more willing to move on if their needs are not met.

Demos research found that only one in four recent graduates expect to be working for the same company in five years' time,[58] while according to some estimates, the average person starting their working life in 2025 will face 19 job changes compared with 13 for those starting out today.[59] However, debates continue about the extent of the change taking place, with some arguing that changes in attitudes are more a reflection of the particular behaviour of people in their twenties and early thirties. That cohort, it is argued, are likely to revert to more traditional models of work when they take on caring and financial responsibilities later in life.[60]

A key challenge for employers and recruiters is to discern how important brands, and issues around ethics and CSR, really are, and what the consequences of ignoring those concerns might be.

Lovely vs lousy jobs

Although 85 per cent of organisations report recruitment difficulties[61] and unemployment levels remain low, it is far from clear that employees with low skill levels exercise anything like the same levels of power and control over their own working lives as those with high skill levels. Low-skilled workers are less likely to benefit from education and training for example – the Leitch Review of Skills reported that highly skilled workers in Britain are five times more likely to be trained at work than low-skilled workers.[62]

According to research done by The Work Foundation 'two thirds of UK workers seem to be enjoying the good life being satisfied or very satisfied with their work. But over four million workers, 15 per cent of the total workforce, are dissatisfied or very dissatisfied with their jobs.'[63] This power gap indicates an important role for government in addressing issues like time off and access to training, where the market fails to take into account wider social aspirations.

A tight vs loose labour market

While employee values and priorities may be changing, their ability to translate their own preferences into new working conditions depends in large part on the current state of the labour market. While unemployment is low employees are far more empowered than in situations where employers have large numbers of employees to choose from (at the moment 87 per cent of the workers that ask for flexible working are granted it[64]). Working conditions, then, are prone to fluctuation unless governments are prepared to intervene through establishing national entitlements to flexible working arrangements and other workplace rights.

5. Technological change

In December 2006 *Time Magazine* announced its 'Person of the year'. Previous winners of the accolade included Pope John Paul II, Bill Gates and Presidents Bush and Clinton. Yet the winner in 2006 was not a world leader, a religious icon, nor a multi-millionaire. It was *You*. The information age is bringing 'an explosion of productivity and innovation',[65] *Time* magazine argued, recognising a generation of people who are exploiting the tools of Web 2.0 – blogs, wikis, videos, feedback – to challenge the pros at their own game.

Over the past ten years, technology has revolutionised the ways in which we relate to – and can collaborate with – one another. It has spawned new social norms, new organisational forms and entirely new business models. Unsurprisingly, this tidal wave of change has burst into recruitment and dramatically changed how things are done.

This chapter explores that change, arguing that:

O   as new technology continues to evolve and its take-up
     becomes more widespread, it looks set to become not only
     a challenge, but an exciting opportunity for the
     recruitment industry over the next decade
O   Web 2.0 offers the opportunity to unleash the value in
     peer-to-peer relationships and active rather than passive
     consumers.

Web 2.0

What *Time* magazine was really describing through its decision was the power of Web 2.0, which has become shorthand for a shift in the way the internet is used and understood. Where in its first phase (the dot.com boom) the web followed an industrial model, where value was still created by experts and organisations and distributed to passive consumers, Web 2.0 turns that model on its head.

Web 2.0 sees the internet as a collaborative tool, where we each have an active role in creating value for one another – whether that is writing a review of a book on Amazon.com, creating an entry on Wikipedia (the online encyclopaedia that readers can edit themselves), or uploading videos onto social networking sites like MySpace and YouTube.

What each of these hugely successful Web 2.0 sites has in common is that they all thrive on the ability to create, nurture and make the best of peer-to-peer *relationships*. The power that can be unlocked through this process has driven some extraordinary business stories in recent years:

- MySpace has 100 million users and is worth US$332.85 million.[66]
- Google is currently valued at US$151.8 billion.[67]
- eBay had revenues of US$4.552 billion in 2005.[68]

Each of these three business models thrives on the active involvement of users, and the relationships that are formed between them. Without this, all three would be entirely content-free. Google aggregates the links that others create on the web; MySpace is nothing more than a set of personal webpages, and eBay is merely a forum for exchange. The users create the content and the value.

As of December 2005, eBay members worldwide have left more than four billion feedback comments for one another regarding their eBay transactions – indicating how an online car-boot sale has become a world-famous brand and leader in its field. People not only buy and sell from one another, they inform each other, rebuke and reward one another.

Web 2.0 meets the recruitment industry

Now, people are using the web for themselves – creating, sharing and editing content. This could be a threat to recruitment, if we didn't work out how to use it.

Interviewee, recruiter

The daily exchanges on eBay or the frivolous videos on YouTube may seem like a long way from the business of recruitment. But just as Web 2.0 business models have penetrated other areas of the economy, we are beginning to see the value of the peer-to-peer relationship – previously exclusive to top-end recruitment – realised across the recruitment industry through the internet.

Simplyhired.com is a vertical search engine company based in Silicon Valley. It is 'building the biggest online database of jobs on the planet'[69] and currently boasts 4,952,453 listings. LinkedIn.com is based on the simple philosophy that relationships matter.[70] It is an online network of more than nine million experienced professionals from around the world, representing 130 industries. Like MySpace for professionals, LinkedIn allows candidates to create a profile that summarises their professional life. Those who have written profiles can find and be found by former colleagues and friends. Your network consists of your connections, your connections' connections, and the people they know – linking you to thousands of professionals worldwide.

We're still a bit funny about career networking online in the UK, but it's huge in the States. The demographics tell an interesting story – the next generation lives life online, professional life won't be any different.

Interviewee, technology expert

LinkedIn and Simply Hired are also connected to one another, in a partnership which integrates business networking with vertical search for the first time, bringing over four million job listings to the LinkedIn jobs network. The result – LinkedIn's 2.5 million users can find inside connections at the companies represented by the job listings. So, if you are a LinkedIn user and you search for a job on Simply Hired, the site shows you if anyone in your network works at the company you would like to work for. The partnership creates the most extensive job search network in the world.

The future? Big general sites will get squeezed out. Small niche sites will grow. Own company websites will get better. Whatever happens it will be online.

Interviewee, advertiser

The internet is increasingly becoming the space where professional life happens. Social networking tools like those adopted by LinkedIn and Simply Hired suggest the capacity of the internet to fundamentally change recruitment into an experience based on collaboration, networking and online engagement.

Zubka.com takes relationships a step further.[71] David Shieldhouse, the founding director of Zubka, explains that while people have referred others for jobs for many years, they have rarely been rewarded for their efforts beyond a warm glow inside. In fact, polling commissioned prior to the launch found that only one in ten people who had successfully recommended another candidate for a job has received any reward for their efforts.

Zubka's business model changes that. It recognises that with the right incentives and rewards, people are willing and able to unlock the enormous value in their personal networks. Zubka's site invites people to refer friends, family and former colleagues for jobs that they think those people will be great at – and, unlike the 90 per cent of people who are not normally rewarded for their efforts, Zubka referrers win a commission when a candidate is successfully placed.

Added to this is the idea that people can recommend others as Zubka referrers and will, in turn, be rewarded for any successful placements that those people make in the future. If it succeeds – and there is every suggestion to think it will – the Zubka workforce could consist of millions of people drawing on their own personal networks and knowledge.

Reaching the passive job seeker

Zubka also exploits another phenomenon bred by the web: the ability to reach passive as well as active customers, people who may not have been aware of a job, or even looking for a move. Log on to Amazon to buy a book and you will immediately be informed which other books you might be interested in, based on the preferences of other people who Amazon believes to have similar taste, or on the basis of your prior behaviour. People all over the world are now buying books that they weren't looking for and possibly had never even heard of only minutes earlier.

Through its referral system, Zubka helps reach the people who aren't typing terms into search engines or leafing through recruitment magazines, but are open to the idea of moving on to a new or more attractive opportunity.

Back-end technology and the recruitment process

Technology at the back end of recruitment is developing rapidly. Scrapers and aggregators are becoming more sensitive, allowing more jobs to be collected in one place. Media sites meanwhile are moving towards offering a personalised service to users which, like the Amazon model, could flag up relevant job ads when they log on.

New technologies allow companies to shift the recruitment process online, often right up to the point of interview. Sensitive psychometric testing, competency questionnaires and verbal and numerical reasoning tests can be designed, administered and scored with very little human input. The data collected after testing can cut candidates based on micro detail – response to a single question, or time taken on a particular section for example.

The most creative companies are matching gaming technology with business scenarios, inviting candidates to simulate a 'day on the job' as part of their recruitment process. Potential BA recruits are asked to turn around a plane in a short space of time, while dealing with a variety of issues – a disabled passenger, late arrivals and airport pressure. Candidates applying for a role at Orange, the mobile phone operator, get hands-on experience of dealing with customers through a call centre simulation – testing their ability to prioritise tasks and deal with difficult customers. These technologies, though still in the early stages, allow candidates to get a feel for what the job will *really* be like, and help employers identify the best people to do the job.

Mobile phones too are set to become influential in recruitment. There are now about 50 million mobile phones in use in the UK.[72] And people who own one are likely to have it with them most of the time. The internet is increasingly accessible via mobile phone, enabling CV release, text messaging for jobs and (limited) jobs site viewing. The constant drive for innovation in recruitment – an effect of the tight labour market – will see the mobile phone pushed to its potential in recruitment over the coming years.

Job advertising

The information revolution has, of course had a huge impact on recruitment advertising. Job advertising continues to move online – and to grow – in large part due to the economics and speed of the web. The cost of advertising online is roughly one-tenth of the price of placing a newspaper ad; and the cost of hiring through the internet costs firms just one-fifth of the standard prices, with the added benefit that all parties can obtain rapid responses.[73]

More than this, though, advertising on the internet is beginning to connect with some of the trends describe in chapter 1 towards greater accountability and clear demonstrations of value. Whereas the value of traditional models of advertising can be difficult to assess (did someone buy a product because they saw it on television?) the web offers opportunities to track customer behaviour.

Job advertising online is still in its infancy, it has a long way to go. The challenge is to stand out, to differentiate yourself – if you don't you won't make any money.

Interviewee, advertiser

Pay-per-click (PPC) advertising is fuelling competitiveness in this area. PPC invites advertisers to bid on keywords they believe their target market would use in a search. The ads show up as sponsored links and sit next to the natural results on a search page. The advertiser pays only when the user clicks on the ad. For example, a search for 'marketing jobs' produces a list of jobs boards and recruitment companies on the main page and Orange, a keen PPC user, in the right hand bar. This technique helps employers direct traffic to their site, rather than to third parties, and in that sense is an important tool for relationship building.

Just as recruitment companies look set to come under increasing pressure to demonstrate value (through tracking retention levels and suitability of matches for example), advertising is becoming far more transparent and accountable. This looks to be an important issue for organisations from all sectors, as efficiency and accountability to either shareholders or taxpayers become priorities.

New technologies coupled with a desire for an increasingly personalised, targeted service leave us with a set of tensions.

Key tensions
Cheap advertising vs information overload

Advertising online may be cheap, and in a market driven by cost efficiency it is easy to see why some would herald the end of more traditional models of reaching people. But it's too soon for that. In fact, the 'paradox of plenty' may push recruitment companies to become the key functionaries in the information age. The problem in an electronic marketplace is not too little information but too much – for candidates keen to avoid endless spam and for those offering jobs intermediaries are needed to help sift through potentially endless amounts of information. The capacity of recruitment companies to digest and process this information for companies and for candidates may become a vital task.

Targeting vs spam

In response to the information overload companies will need to identify better ways of reaching people. Using technology to identify and target certain groups is one approach; another is for a trusted brand – perhaps a recruitment agency – to act as an intermediary, supplying active and passive job seekers with regular, *relevant* and timely updates on opportunities available to them, and filtering candidate information back to employers.

Efficiency vs judgement for companies

There is a limit to what technology can do, and many employers remain sceptical of tools that aspire to remove the individual from the recruitment process almost completely.

According to one interviewee: 'Recruitment is an art – recognising skills, experience and fit are fundamental to getting the right person for a job. Fit means understanding the company *and* the individual. A computer can't do that.'

Intangible 'soft' skills, like the ability to work in a team and be creative, are ever more important to employers. While simulations can go some way to identifying these skills, ultimately human judgement will remain imperative.

Brand and the recruitment experience vs automation

Equally, candidate perceptions of the business are proving more and more important. Walking the talk matters – even in the recruitment process itself. Employer brand and the recruitment experience are closely linked – and organisations must decide for themselves the extent to which they want to automate recruitment processes when those processes themselves can be an opportunity to sell the merits of a job opportunity to a potential employee.

Part 2:
Challenges to old
business models

6. Challenges to old business models

Some of the tension in writing this pamphlet has not only been describing an industry that is changing very quickly, but also in the historic division between two models of recruitment.

Two models of recruitment

One of these models has been the extremely personalised, high-level recruitment practices used to fill highly skilled, highly paid jobs. And the second approach has been an industrial model used to fill low-skilled vacancies – in which big companies, employing lots of people, offered a large number of relatively standardised jobs.

In the first of these models value was created in *relationships* – between clients and recruitment companies; between candidates and companies; in peer-to-peer networks that recruitment companies made use of. In the second model, value was created in *institutions* by employees of recruitment companies matching candidates with vacancies, using powerful databases. This contrast is set out in table 2.

With the advent of the internet large parts of the recruitment industry shifted online – driven by the economics and speed of the internet. Jobs sites – like Monster, Fish4Jobs and Totaljobs – took over many agency and advertiser functions, doing traditional tasks quicker, cheaper and with more transparency.

But the internet remained a tool for one-way transmission – offering employers a new *space* to advertise their jobs and identify

Table 1 Two models of recruitment

Highly skilled jobs (highly personalised service)	Low-skilled jobs (more standardised service)
Specific role to be filled	Generic roles to be filled
Certified skills required *plus tacit judgements about suitability*	Certified skills required
Low volume, high cost	High volume, low cost
Identify candidates through networks and peer-to-peer recommendation	Identify candidates through database
Candidate pool from active *and* passive job seekers (people approached about jobs)	Candidate pool from active job seekers only (people looking for jobs)
Candidate interest in pay *plus wider set of factors about role and organisation (progression, company ethic etc)*	Candidate interest in pay
Build relationships with clients and candidates	Functional communication when necessary

candidates, not a fundamentally new *way* to approach their roles.

However, this continuity is already being challenged: the gap between the two models is being challenges by two sets of factors:

O   new expectations
O   new opportunities.

New expectations

Chapters 1–5 of this pamphlet describe the way in recruitment companies are having to contend with new expectations from a number of angles.

The drive for **talent** has pushed companies to think about what they *need*, rather than what they need *right now*. Identifying, attracting, employing and developing the right people are key parts of the recruitment process in the world's most successful companies – this is the war for talent.

This war marks part of a bigger shift in company focus – an emphasis on **value** rather than **cost**. Driven by efficiency, companies are seeking new ways of generating value. One of these, identified by a number of top companies, is taking the recruitment process back in-house – focusing on long-term strategic investment in people, rather than quick-fix solutions.

Brand is increasingly tied up with business identity and perceptions of success, driving organisations to reflect on their image in the marketplace. People – often the external face of an organisation – have taken on greater significance, as employers recognise their ability to determine market perception.

Reflecting on this, employers are placing more value on who they recruit, and how that person fits the brand and **culture of the organisation**. In an increasingly competitive environment, brand differentiation among competitors is imperative. This has a direct impact on the recruitment *process*, as organisations move towards **recruiting on the basis of** *behaviours*, rather than certified competencies alone. These behaviours, identified and prioritised by an organisation, indicate that candidates do things 'the company way'. They demonstrate synergy with company values and brand, as well as straightforward ability to get the job done.

Personal ethics and values are increasingly bound up with people's choice of job and employer. Priorities and expectations of work have shifted – **employees want company ethos** to reflect their own values set, and cite corporate social responsibility as a key part of the *employer* selection process.

The boundaries between the personal and the professional have also undergone a significant shift. Now, the terms and conditions of a 'good job' go well beyond pay – companionship, **fulfilment and quality of life** have become basic employee expectations of work.

These changes indicate a shift in the relationship between employee and employer – from a traditional contract based on capital in exchange for labour, to an accord between two parties reflecting the needs and aspirations of both.

New opportunities

Web 2.0 has opened recruitment up – two-way information flows, social networking, peer-to-peer, feedback and transparency – and invited employers and employees to engage with one another on a new platform.

In the knowledge economy information is power. Web 2.0 collects this power and allows it to be reviewed, shared, altered, discussed and responded to in an open space. But too much information leads to confusion and apathy. Powerful technologies – using material generated by Web 2.0 – create **personalised responses** to individual needs. Using search engines, scrapers and aggregators, Web 2.0 gives employees *and* employers exactly what they want, filtering out junk and responding to an identified and articulated need.

This information is increasingly used to develop **relationships** – primarily between employer and candidate – which may lead to a job. But **peer-to-peer** is where Web 2.0 is adding real value. Bringing individuals together – to exchange knowledge or recommendations – challenges traditional professionalism, and shifts the balance of power in favour of the individual.

These changes, combined with the transparency inherent to the internet and the feedback mechanisms exclusive to Web 2.0, encourage individuals to evaluate employers, and invites employers to view the personal and professional histories of a potential employee – the deeper challenges associated with this trend will be addressed in the next chapter.

Technology also breeds opportunities for much greater **accountability in advertising** – with the advent of payment per click shifting the emphasis of much advertising away from speculative (if still strategic) advertising, to data-rich, accountable spending on the part of companies – where **payment happens by results**.

The increasingly complex relationship between employers and employees – reflected in the changing demands described above –

also creates opportunities for recruitment companies to consider how else they can add value **not just as suppliers of specific services, but also as intermediaries** in labour markets. In a world where brand and reputation are becoming increasingly important, the ability to help companies learn about how they are perceived in the labour market – and how attractive their offer is to potential candidates – becomes more and more valuable.

Beyond the industrial model

The changes brought about by these new expectations and new opportunities are closing the gap between the two models described above. Many of the approaches traditionally applied in high-level recruitment are filtering through to lower skilled jobs as employers and individuals become more sophisticated in their decision-making and new business models make that affordable.

In general terms this suggests a move away from standardisation towards a model which values distinctiveness and individuality. Value is created by users – employers and employees – and networks replace databases as the central source of information. Openness and transparency – core principles of the new model – breed accountability, allowing employers *and* employees to hold one another to account. Service providers too – agencies and advertisers – are accountable, as efficiency demands tight evaluation procedures and ongoing feedback. Technology is vital to the new model, as personalised, targeted services replace the one-size-fits-all approach of the past. Talent, rather than availability, is the driver of the model putting the individual – their experience, aspirations and expectations – at the very centre of the process.

The following section makes a series of recommendations, based on the principles of the business model outlined above.

Ensure that commissioning processes focus on value rather than cost

Efficiency and accountability are at the centre of the new business model. In a world where organisations want to know not just what service they are buying, but what *value* a third party organisation can provide, finding ways to demonstrate genuine impact is paramount.

Track retention and demonstrate impact

Tracking the origin of staff – via agency, employee referral or online recruitment campaign – and monitoring their levels of retention is becoming more common. Slowly, organisations are recognising the value of monitoring behaviours and experiences, particularly during an employee's first year. Mapping the employee journeys allows companies to match experience with outcome, establishing what helped to engage the best people, and what failed. Recruitment agencies and employers themselves ought to adapt their evaluation processes in response to this challenge. Inviting clients to evaluate them based on certain criteria would allow agencies to lead on change in this area.

Demand accountable advertising online to demonstrate impact

In the same way in which third party recruitment looks set to be affected by the drive for leanness, accountability and efficiency, so too does advertising on the web. Traffic to websites and online behaviour are increasingly easy to track. Pay-per-click (PPC) advertising allows companies to direct job seekers to their website via a standard search.

Once there companies can evaluate how people behave – using the information to inform future design and process. This technology has the potential to change the market completely – in future, companies might pay advertisers only on the basis of responses they receive to an ad, or on how many candidates get through their screening process. Ultimately, they may hand over a fee only once a job is filled. Advertisers must stay ahead of the trend here, working out innovative ways to remain competitive, despite tighter accountability structures.

Help organisations learn about themselves by overcoming the insider/outsider problem

In a world in which ethos, ethics, branding and reputation are becoming more important than ever in recruiting and retaining staff, recruitment companies – as intermediaries between employers and the labour market – can become the eyes and ears of their clients.

Organisations suffer when they develop an insider/outsider problem: when the way they see themselves and the way the rest of the world sees them are incompatible. An organisation may believe that it is living – and communicating – its values when, in fact, its reputation in the labour market and wider society suggests that it is being far less successful in this respect.

The opportunity for recruitment companies is that they are in an ideal position not just to find and place candidates – but to help organisations learn about themselves and how they are perceived. Delivering high-quality candidates will remain a non-negotiable, but becoming a resource for feedback and learning offers a new opportunity for recruiters to create value for clients.

Align human resources, public relations and marketing and be clear on core organisational values

Rapid and regular information exchange among users online means – despite impressive advertising campaigns – organisations have less control over their brand. Having a core set of values, which reflect the brand but are lived by the company and its employees, may be a more powerful way of telling an effective story about an organisation and what it stands for.

Telling this story means joining up functions in-house. HR, PR and Marketing – with overlapping responsibilities in respect of brand – should align their strategies in order to convey brand values more effectively.

Align the recruitment experience with client ethos

At a time when job seekers are showing an increasing interest not just in levels of pay but also in a much wider set of factors – including how it *feels* to work somewhere – the experience of being recruited matters.

Organisations with a relaxed, business-like or playful ethos (and brand) need to ensure that the process of recruitment itself reflects that ethos. When candidates go through recruitment processes they are also gathering information and making judgements about their potential employers – meaning that the process must reflect the organisation itself. This requires differentiated processes designed not just to identify the right competencies but also to create the right impression.

Find ways to connect with the passive job seeker

For years the bulk of recruitment has dealt with people *actively looking* for a job. People have joined agencies – and those agencies have helped people find jobs. The market for active job seekers will always be important and valuable, but connecting with the *passive* job seeker represents an entirely new set of opportunities.

The business models described in chapter 5 can be understood as the efforts of the early adopters in of this approach. Organisations like Zubka, LinkedIn and Simply Hired work through the power and reach of the network, rather than the sum of the knowledge within an organisation. Personal referrals not only tap into the rich knowledge that we all have of our peers and acquaintances, but also provide ways for organisations to reach them when they may not be actively looking for a job. This potentially expands an organisation's reach and knowledge – and talent pool – enormously.

Future recruiters and businesses will identify the passive job seeker long before he or she applies for a job. They will track his interest and maintain a light-touch relationship, keeping him up to date on company news. Their sensitive search engine will match her to jobs as they come up, and let her know they're interested in her application. When he is ready for a change he will log his interest with them and they will respond. This is more than a quick transaction, it is a relationship built up over time, based on mutual interest and understanding. To maximise their talent pool HR departments and recruitment agencies should use technology to connect with passive job seekers in this way.

Broker and utilise peer-to-peer relationships

Slowly organisations across sectors are beginning to identify the value that lies in peer-to-peer relationships. Online 'communities' are an obvious example of this, while offline experiments with peer support, mentoring and social events are key ways for large organisations to add value. Beyond simply *drawing* on these relationships, however, there is an opportunity for recruitment organisations to help *connect* people to one another.

Use Web 2.0 to build personalised relationships online

A central feature of Web 2.0 is the opportunity to develop online relationships with – and services to – individuals that become more personalised over time. Log on to Amazon.com and you will be advised which other books you might like to read, on the basis of the choices made by others or previous choices made by you. Explore the site further and you can adjust your profile to make this advice more accurate and useful in the future. Log on to Pandora.com and you can create your own personalised radio station – building up a profile by rating songs that the site suggests you should listen to.

These features are transferable to recruitment. Users should be able to actively shape their own profiles and relationships online – allowing content to come to them without having to contend with endless spam. Building these feedback mechanisms into online activity and alerting people to the choices made by others hold the potential of far more personalised relationships to be built up over time at minimal cost.

Tap into the long tail

The rise of advertising online raises some interesting challenges and opportunities for the industry. On the one hand advertising online brings in less money per advert for those selling advertising space, but the internet offers unlimited space – and is more affordable to a greater number of organisations.

While the cost *per advert* may therefore be less online, there may

Figure 13 The marketplace

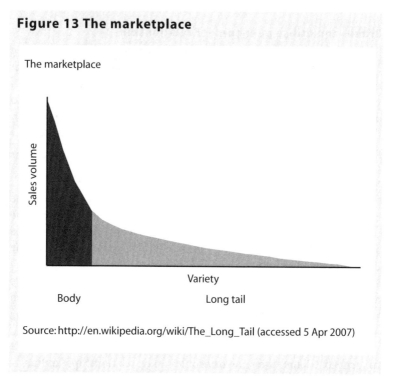

Source: http://en.wikipedia.org/wiki/The_Long_Tail (accessed 5 Apr 2007)

well also be *many more* adverts placed in total – opening up the opportunity for many more 'niche' adverts to be placed in the future.

This is what Chris Anderson, the editor of *Wired Magazine*, has described as the long tail. He argues that the web offers the opportunity to go beyond the 'tyranny of the big hit', noting that Google makes most of its money from small advertisers rather than blockbuster advertising placements by one company at any one time. As Kevin Laws, an American venture capitalist, argues, 'The biggest money is in the smallest sales.'[74]

Anderson argues that the long tail (see figure 13) relies on more than just space and economics, however. He offers three key principles:

Rule 1: *Make everything available.*
Rule 2: *Cut the price in half. Now lower it.*
Rule 3: *Help me find it.*

The third of these principles is vital: 'everything available' can easily become 'information overload' without ways of aggregating information, directing people and filtering out unwanted information. This points towards the importance of many of the tools of Web 2.0 – and of recruitment agencies as intermediaries – in helping people navigate the long tail.

Part 3:
Social challenges beyond the market

7. Social challenges beyond the market

One of the core themes running through this pamphlet has been both the ingenuity and the shortcomings of markets.

The trends we have described, and the ways in which they might interact with one another in the future, will present huge challenges – many of which will be overcome through the market. New social values will filter through into corporate decision-making and behaviour; changing demographics will tilt the focus of those operating in the market closer towards those groups that currently suffer employment penalties; new technology will probably give rise to business models that no one has even thought of yet as people identify new opportunities to create value.

Yet for all their uses, markets often produce imperfect results. They can produce disparities in power that undermine people's ability to shape their own lives. Their outcomes can overlap with social goals, such as more inclusive workplaces, without ever fully achieving them. And markets can be very poor forums for *collective* decisions about the kind of society that we want to live in; the sum of our individual choices often produces outcomes that none of us are comfortable with.

This chapter explores some of those shortcomings, raising a set of distinctly *social* concerns and offering recommendations for government and others to help address them. Some of the issues touched on in this pamphlet are not discussed here – helping the *whole population* access education and training in adult life, and finding ways to support work–life balance are vital issues, but deserve more attention than can be offered to them here. They are already the focus of specific pieces of work at Demos, and will be the subject of further published reports in 2007.

Keeping our focus on recruitment, we make recommendations in three specific areas:

- O making markets work for people
- O helping organisations to diversify their workforces
- O addressing privacy in the information age.

Making markets work for people

The foundation of capitalism is the promise of the future: the promise of repeat business with existing customers, or further business with new customers. Game theory tells us that we will work co-operatively with others when we know the decisions that we make today will affect us in the future[75] and nowhere does this apply more than to markets. Reputable companies provide good services and therefore win future contracts, or disreputable companies provide poor services and do not.

Future business success therefore is the risk of poor or unethical performance. This reality was captured neatly in a remark made by BP Chairman Lord Browne in an interview with the *Spectator* in May 2006. He commented: 'Our values are to do business in such a way that it can be done again and again. It is very unwise to think that anything is the last transaction.'[76]

Lord Browne's remark was seized on in some quarters as proof that capitalism will, after all, regulate itself. Adam Smith's modern-day representatives described the comment as 'a remark that so neatly says what capitalism is really about, rather than what its critics think it is about'.[77]

The difficulty, however, is that this is not necessarily true. Because Lord Browne was not describing what capitalism is all about – but rather what it *can* and *should* be like – when the right conditions are in place. In a market with strong information, consequences for unethical behaviour, and a realistic set of alternative options, it *is* unwise to think that anything is the last transaction.

However, in markets with poor information and few consequences for unethical action the dynamics change. This truth – that markets can function either effectively or ineffectively – is reflected in the rather more nuanced interpretation of how markets work provided by another man who has made millions – Pierre Omidyar, the founder of eBay.

His short explanation of the idea behind his multi-million dollar company contains this:

> *Most people are honest. And they mean well. But some people are dishonest. Or deceptive. This is true here, in the newsgroups, in the classifieds, and right next door. It's a fact of life. But here, those people can't hide. We'll drive them away. Use our feedback forum. Give praise where it is due; make complaints where appropriate.*[78]

What the founder of eBay has done has been to find a way of ensuring that more people behave ethically, by strengthening feedback loops that can be weak in markets with a poor sense of the future.

eBay provides this sense of the future through its peer-to-peer feedback system. eBay users provide star ratings and written feedback on others who they have traded with, collectively building up a picture of who else in the market is efficient, trustworthy and reliable. Those who perform well are rewarded with a strong (clear) reputation, while those who perform poorly or unethically are likely to be driven away as Omidyar describes.

Through doing this, eBay has become both a free market and a highly regulated one – because information is so rich that people within the market become everyday regulators. Activists can exist within markets as well as within civil society. And the truly important point here is that the information provided by these everyday activists captures the *experience* of working with a company, rather than merely a set of credentials that they lay claim to. Because while credentials can be an important indicator of compliance with minimum standards, companies understandably want *excellence* rather than a guarantee of a basic minimum when they are making decisions as important as who to employ.

This offers an important lesson for those interested in improving the overall quality and reputation of the recruitment industry.

We recommend that leading players in the industry should find a way of creating an eBay-style site to help provide information and feedback to future clients of the industry. This web tool could incorporate much of the work that has already been done to provide clear information – bringing together feedback and reviews from customers with accreditation and other evidence of strong future credentials such as ethical pledges. Taking eBay as its model, this approach would seek to combine the dynamism of an open market with the information, feedback loops and sense of the future required to make that work.

Helping organisations to diversify their workforces

It has become commonplace to argue that there is a generic business case for diversity in organisations. In a comprehensive study published in 2004, the Institute for Public Policy Research identified the following benefits to building an ethnically diverse workforce:

○ a broader recruitment pool (talent)
○ meeting customer needs
○ the creative mix
○ access to government business
○ public reputation
○ building a modern brand
○ access to a growing small and medium enterprise (SME) marketplace.[79]

Such benefits looks persuasive, particularly when set alongside demographic trends which show that 8 per cent of the workforce will be from a minority ethnic group by 2030. Beyond ethnicity, there is also good evidence to suggest that open and inclusive organisations will be best placed to attract and retain staff with a range of personal backgrounds. The campaigning group Stonewall, for example, has found that 36 per cent of gay employees will change careers if discrimination is continued.[80] The numbers of men and women at work are almost equal in the UK, highlighting the importance of workplaces that are welcoming of both men and women.

As a 2006 Recruitment and Employment Confederation (REC) report on the recruitment industry – undertaken in association with Ernst and Young – suggested, 'with changing demographics in the UK, recruiters' very business success will increasingly depend on their ability to reach out to the widest possible candidate market'.[81] In this sense, one thing is clear: there certainly appear to be few downsides to employing a diverse range of employees.

Highlighting the 'business case' that appears to stem from these benefits is a comfortable position for politicians to adopt (it absolves them of responsibility for diversity beyond providing businesses with information and stamping out clear cases of racism and discrimination); it is a fortuitous position for businesses and business lobby groups to take up (it absolves them from more legislation to comply with and is, in fairness, true in some cases); and it is a natural position for campaigning groups seeking to promote social inclusion (it fits with their own values and worldview).

However a crucial question is whether, given the painfully slow progress towards workplaces *actually becoming more diverse*, such a business case exists in practice and for all businesses. Because while *employing* a more diverse workforce may be beneficial to businesses, achieving that in practice can involve considerable time, effort – and money.

A glimpse at best practice in recruiting to promote diversity indicates this. An organisation seeking to diversify its workforce might decide to advertise in a range of places – not just on its own website but in the minority ethnic press, or the *Pink Paper* for example. This can be an important way of sending an unambiguous message that people from all backgrounds are welcome and wanted. It might also train its employees to conduct interviews and put together advertising that supports this message. And it might spend time running work experience schemes, or organising events in the community to illustrate its inclusive culture.

All of this costs money – often more money than is available to SMEs acting alone. Many SMEs simply do not have the same economies of scale available to investment banks or large retailers, who are able to spend relatively large amounts of money – yet devote relatively small proportions of their overall turnover – on these activities.

Given this discrepancy, perhaps it should not be surprising that ippr's taskforce found that 'many SMEs do not see a business case for race equality and diversity in their workforce: 60 per cent of our respondents did not have formal race equality or equal opportunities strategies in place'.[82]

The interpretation of this finding by the (business-led) taskforce was that more information was needed to illustrate the benefits of diversity. Businesses would see sense with just a little more education. However, the harsh reality that emerged from our own interviews – and which is clearly shown in the statistical employment penalties shown in chapter 3 – is that for many businesses the costs of recruiting for diversity can outweigh the undoubted business benefits of actually achieving it.

In other words there is a market failure for diversity: many businesses that would, in an ideal world, like to diversify their workforces, cannot find the time or resources to do so. Instead they settle for hiring those who can be recruited easily and at low cost, through networks or conventional channels.

This rarely spoken of reality can create a negative feedback loop, in which inaction leads to very slow progress . . . leading to further inaction.

Yet while the market cannot be relied on to provide the nation with diverse workplaces, we know that diversity in the workplace is of increasing social importance. At a time where social cohesion and social inclusion are major concerns, the workplace – where many people spend five out of seven days every week – is a crucial site for everyday interaction and integration.

Any debate about a role for government in this area requires an injection of realism and some conceptual clarity about the reasons to aspire towards a more diverse workforce at a national level.[83] In social terms, it is possible to identify four key reasons to aspire towards diverse workforces:

- *business benefits*: solving collective action problems, helping businesses of all shapes and sizes access talent, forge strong links with supply chains, avoid homogeneity and create strong reputations with their customer base and communities
- *social justice*: recognising that diverse workforces are a reflection of a meritocratic society, where opportunities are not dependent on personal and social status
- *representation*: taking action to make public institutions more genuinely representative to provide role models, legitimacy and reassurance to all communities in the UK
- *social cohesion*: understanding workplaces as a sight for social integration and interaction.

Each of these reasons has their own logic, but the difficulty is that the reasons – even within the categories assigned above – are not perfectly overlapping. An organisation can be meritocratic without being representative, or visa versa. An organisation can avoid homogeneity without being genuinely diverse. Organisations might access all the talent available but end up becoming very homogenous, contributing little to integration, and so on.

Any policy measures or other interventions designed to tackle the market failure for diversity should be clear about their own rationale for promoting diversity – and of how they plan to affect behaviour.

We recommend that businesses should be given support in diversifying their workforces – because SMEs all around the country need help in this area and because the country as a whole would benefit in becoming a fairer, more socially integrated society. As the Prime Minister's Strategy Unit has written:

> *The task of promoting the economic integration of ethnic minority groups through labour market inclusion is intimately linked with the long-term aim of promoting social, cultural, civil and political integration. . . . The limited economic integration of some ethnic minority groups can be linked with, and lead to, greater signs of isolation and alienation from the norms of society as a whole.*[84]

The trend over the last century has been towards more legislation – and there is a legitimate debate around whether the private sector should be exempt from duties placed on the public sector. However, as the interim report of the Equalities Commission found, legal measures have had some positive effects but have not been sufficient in tackling the problem alone.[85] Similarly, while appeals to companies' sense of 'social responsibility' will do no harm, the rate of progress to date suggests a more systematic approach based on reducing the costs of promoting diversity should be adopted.

Given this finding – and the difficulty in pinning down a definition of diversity – the goal of government should therefore be to help businesses become as open and inclusive as possible.

One clear way in which to take this forward would be through the nationwide network of sector skills councils (SSCs). These organisations – which cover 85 per cent of the British workforce[86] – are in a position to take an overview of their own sectors and to support employers in reaching and attracting people from a much greater range of backgrounds.

As things stand, sector skills councils are set four key goals:

O to reduce skills gaps and shortages
O to improve productivity, business and public performance
O to increase opportunities to boost the skills and productivity of everyone in the sector's workforce

o   to improve learning supply including apprenticeships, higher education and National Occupational Standards (NOS).[87]

We recommend that a fifth core goal should be added:

o   *to attract the widest possible pool of talent into the industry – involving new and different people from all backgrounds to work and prosper in the sector.*

In this way, SSCs could not only perform a useful business function for smaller companies in particular, but would be responsible for helping to deliver an important set of wider social goals. This is not to suggest a course of positive discrimination, but rather a concerted programme of *positive action* from sector to sector (an important distinction, which is described in box 3).

Box 3 Positive action

Positive action seeks to increase the number of candidates for positions – and is an approach already adopted by organisations across the public and private sector. It does not seek to judge candidates on their background, but rather to encourage potential candidates from all backgrounds to put themselves forward with confidence. In this sense, it is often used to address the image of an organisation or industry, or to build the confidence of an individual or community.

Positive discrimination, however, deliberately takes an individual's background into consideration in selection procedures, as a means to address past discrimination or on the basis that the challenge of diversifying a workforce is so intractable that it requires a change to the rules.

While positive discrimination is unlawful in the UK, positive action is lawful and has much wider public support.

The value of setting a broad outcome goal for SSCs of attracting the widest possible pool of talent into a sector's workforce would be to encourage innovation within and between sectors: diversifying workforces in banking is likely to be a different proposition from achieving the same goal in a small, highly networked sectors.

In broad terms, however, SSCs would be expected to focus their efforts on supporting SMEs, through measures like advertising campaigns, staging recruitment fairs and events in disadvantaged areas and potentially match-funding diversity training or schemes designed to provide work experience placements.

Under these new arrangements, sector skills councils could be held to account by government against progress made, while providing an institutional focus for collaboration between charities, campaigning groups and business organisations.

Addressing privacy in the information age

Ten years ago making an application for a job was a discreet process. An application would be sent and received. A professional interview would take place. References with previous *employers* would be taken up and a job would either be offered – or not – based on that set of professional interactions.

In 2007, however, we are all becoming searchable. Typing someone's name into Google can be at least as informative as the information that an individual provides in a CV or covering letter. *What are they really like*, we wonder. Just as companies lose control of their brands in the information age, the terms of a conversation with a future employer are no longer restricted to what we choose to talk about in an interview.

And what is more, Google sees no distinction between personal and private lives. Searching for someone on the internet is just as likely to find the photographs of last year's office party as our professional achievements. Add to this the fact that *other people* may have posted up those photos without us even knowing – and that once content is up on the internet it can be impossible to remove it altogether – and suddenly applying for a job looks a far more complicated prospect.

The evidence is beginning to mount to suggest that this is already affecting recruitment decisions. According to research from the United States, three out of four recruiters undertake internet research on candidates and one in four has dropped candidates based on what the searches found.[88]

Meanwhile, job applicants themselves are beginning to identify their internet trails as potential obstacles to employment. Forty-seven per cent of college grad job seekers who use social networking sites such as MySpace and Facebook have either already changed or plan to change the content of their pages as a result of their job search.[89]

The likelihood is that in the medium to long term we will simply adjust to this level of transparency accepting that employees can have personal lives which have little or no effect on their ability to work effectively.

However, the generation entering the labour market in the next five years may be in for a rocky ride as society makes the transition. Today's teenagers – the 'digital natives' – are those who have embraced the openness and self-expression of the internet, growing up with it as a normal part of their lives. Entering the working world – or at least trying to – where this level of openness is not yet the norm may be a culture shock.

We recommend that the careers advisers in schools and universities alert young people to the potential dangers to their career that could be caused by this culture clash between high levels of openness and often relatively closed organisational cultures.

The internet by its nature cannot be regulated but people can certainly regulate their own behaviour when they are made aware of the possible consequences of their actions in the future.

Conclusion

When asked what she thought she had changed during her time as prime minister, Margaret Thatcher gave a reply that has since become famous: 'everything'.[90] This of course ignored questions as to whether 'Thatcherism' was the symptom or the cause of huge social change in that period. Nevertheless, what is clear is that as the twentieth century drew to an end, Adam Smith's 'invisible hand' had never been more visible. The West, including Thatcher's Britain, had decided that it could not live without the market. With that choice settled, however, individuals, businesses and nations all around the world are faced with an equally important concern of *how to live with* the market.

In business and in the labour market, organisations and individuals are coming to terms with a new set of sweeping changes across society, from mass migration and global competition to the rise of new technology. These changes are altering the demands that are made on organisations, the opportunities open to people and the nature of the workforce itself.

And politically, both the left and the right in Britain are adjusting to a new era in which a market economy has become part of the mainstream, but the answer to *what kind of market economy* remains both contested and uncertain. Huge questions remain as to how to ensure that markets are fair and efficient, that people are best equipped to thrive within them and that as a society we are able to identify social challenges that will never be addressed through the market alone – however well it functions.

This pamphlet has aimed to contribute to answering those questions by doing three things:

O   first, offering a guide to those operating in the market for recruitment, from employers and recruitment companies to job seekers themselves, to the important trends shaping society – and their likely implications

O   second, suggesting ways of improving the efficiency and fairness of the market for recruitment companies by giving that market a clearer sense of the future

O   third, identifying a key set of social challenges which we believe will not be met through the market – and making recommendations designed to help address those challenges.

Our argument

We have argued that the traditional divide between extremely personalised recruitment for highly skilled jobs and relatively standardised recruitment processes for low-skilled jobs looks set to close in the coming years. A combination of new expectations and new opportunities, we suggest, will drive a more personalised approach across the spectrum.

Our recommendations
Beyond the traditional model

We make a series of recommendations to support this process.
Employers should:

1   ensure that commissioning processes – whether through HR or procurement – focus on value rather than cost

2   align HR, PR and marketing and be clear about core organisational values.

Recruitment professionals should:

1   track retention to demonstrate impact
2   demand accountable advertising online to demonstrate impact
3   help organisations learn about themselves by overcoming the insider/outsider problem
4   align the recruitment experience with client ethos
5   find ways to connect with the passive job seeker
6   broker and utilise peer-to-peer relationships
7   use Web 2.0 to build personalised relationships online
8   tap into the long tail.

Markets and social policy

The theme running throughout this pamphlet is both the ingenuity and shortcomings of markets. We argue that many of the likely changes in the market for recruitment will have positive consequences. However, for all their uses, markets often produce imperfect results. They can produce disparities in power which undermine people's ability to shape their own lives. Their outcomes can overlap with social goals, such as more inclusive workplaces, without ever fully achieving them. And markets can be very poor forums for *collective* decisions about the kind of society that we want to live in; the sum of our individual choices often produces outcomes that none of us are comfortable with.

We have identified three social challenges that we consider *beyond the market,* and keeping our focus on recruitment we make recommendations for:

O   *making markets work for people*: through an eBay-style system of self-regulation and peer-to-peer feedback
O   *helping organisations diversify their workforces*: through adding a fifth core goal to sector skills councils' remit – 'to attract the widest possible pool of talent into the industry

– involving new and different people from all
backgrounds to work and prosper in the sector'

O   *addressing privacy in the information age*: through advising
young people about potential dangers to their career that
could be caused by this culture clash between high levels
of openness on websites like YouTube.com and the
relatively closed organisational cultures of the corporate
world.

A word on the future

A core principle behind scenario planning is that it is impossible to
predict an inherently unpredictable future. That same uncertainty,
however, should be empowering. The uncertainty surrounding the
future highlights the possibility of many different future scenarios –
and signals our own ability as individuals, organisations and whole
societies to shape change as we would prefer it.

We hope that the research, analysis and recommendations contained in this pamphlet go some way to helping all those with a stake
in the recruitment process and help create a future that is brighter,
happier and more productive.

Appendix: Scenarios

Over the past 50 years scenarios have become an increasingly important tool for helping decision-makers to formulate well-informed, long-term strategies.

The purpose of the scenario is **absolutely not to predict the future** – and none of the four scenarios here should be interpreted as such. Rather, scenarios are used to explore the implications of present trends and future possibilities, in order to prepare for any number of potential futures.

In this sense, scenarios are designed to prepare us for inherently unpredictable events – and to provide us with the information we need to shape the future through our own decisions. Box 4 outlines how this methodology has been successfully employed across the globe.

> *Box 4 Uses of scenario planning around the world*
>
> Under the guidance of the futures expert Peter Schwartz, Shell famously used scenario planning to identify the possibility of an oil crisis in the early 1970s. When the crisis actually happened, Shell was able to weather the storm much better than its competitors. Shell negotiated the various obstacles of the 1970s

and 1980s to become one of the top oil-producing companies in the world.

Scenarios soon became a topic of great interest to businesses and governments around the world. Recently the British government undertook a major health review using scenario planning to study the long-term trends affecting the UK health service. The review prompted a shift within health policy towards public health and preventative approaches (such as tackling smoking, obesity and excessive salt consumption). The Department for Trade and Industry (DTI) and the Prime Minister's Strategy Unit are leading on the use of scenarios in government in the UK.

The four scenarios used in this report were developed through a process designed by Demos and used regularly in our work. The process drew on knowledge from across the recruitment industry – advertisers, agencies, academics and employers. A workshop at Demos mid-way through the research process invited expert opinions to contribute to our research. The process for designing the scenarios involved four stages:

1   identifying key trends affecting the recruitment
     industry:
     O   over the last ten years
     O   over the next ten years
2   identifying important and uncertain factors
3   developing sketch scenarios
4   finalising scenarios.

Figure 14 shows the starting point for developing the scenarios. We identified changes in technology and the economic climate as two key critical uncertainties, and these were used as the basis for our scenarios. The four scenarios have been included to provide background to the report and the research process, and as a stimulus for discussion over the coming years.

Figure 14 Scenarios

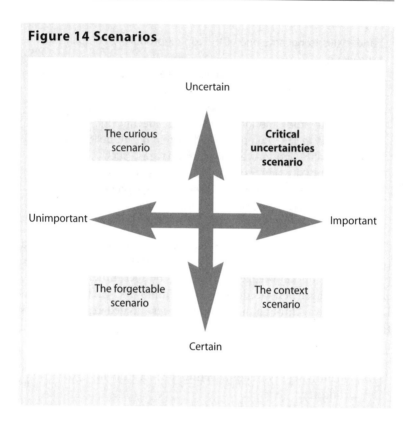

Choice utopia (disruptive technological progress and an employee-driven market)

Google enters recruitment, sending shockwaves through the corporate world, recruitment companies and sites online. Recruitment companies and advertisers were worried when the government set up its own free-to-use site in 2010, but soon realised that the real dynamism and competition would come from the Web 2.0 businesses as companies voted with their feet.

Now that everyone's CV is online, the searchability provided by Google means that employers can find employees more easily than ever before. More than this though, they can also *find out about each other*. In this brave new world of technology everything seems to be available online: job seekers' personal lives, employees' experiences of work, and every detail imaginable about companies themselves.

All this puts powerful graduates in the driving seat, allowing them to decide who they work for based on brands, ethics and generous working conditions as well as their basic salary. The backlash against immigration has also helped force wages up in the burgeoning service sector, gradually helping to close the gap between 'lovely' and 'lousy' jobs.

Recruiters laugh that it is employees with all the power – not them or even their clients. They adapt to the challenge of new technology by trading on personal relationships, tacit judgement and 'the human touch' in the recruitment process. Some firms re-brand themselves as 'HR solutions' providers, taking over all the HR operations of their clients.

If you find it its yours (incremental technological progress and an employee-driven market)

After 20 years of unprecedented growth there are plenty of jobs to go around. Many felt that the government's 'open door' immigration policy would see job opportunities drying up, but Britain is reaping the benefits of globalisation and its economy is booming.

Generation Y. They confounded the expectations that they would grow out of their attitudes to work later in life. They look for 'experiences' in work – and are willing to go somewhere else if their employer stops providing them. For many, the idea of a career has become an anachronism.

Meanwhile, the older generation dips in and out of the job market, topping up their pensions with part-time work and one-off jobs. 'Grey recruitment' is a lucrative – and important – business.

In the 2010s technology continued to improve, becoming more reliable, with new software providing a reassuring level of privacy for job seekers. But in many ways companies are using it to do the same old things quicker and more efficiently.

With a strong economy, a tight labour market, and only incremental improvements in technology, it seems that everyone is relying on recruitment companies. Margins have risen back to the levels of the early 2000s, as companies have little trouble trading on their knowledge, networks and expertise.

Take what you can get (incremental technological progress and an employer-driven market)

The economy has taken a downturn and there are fewer jobs to go around, but immigration has continued apace. There is high competition for all jobs, and the market is flooded with graduates who have high expectations but few opportunities to use their skills.

The flexible nature of the labour market means that retention is more a concern for employees than employers, and once in work people are battling to keep their jobs. The autonomy of employees that was familiar in the early 2000s is all but a distant memory. Now, investing in skills is a low priority for employers. They can choose what to spend their money on, while still reeling in the best people, who remain on the outside, desperate for work.

The initial excitement about Web 2.0 and complicated database management tools has subsided. Filtering people through the internet was a short-lived phenomenon. Employers reported more failure than success from this approach, and have almost without exception shifted away from it, citing the human touch as the most important element in recruitment.

But despite the technology threat waning, recruitment agencies continue to face uncertainty. The downturn in the economy means more companies are developing tighter business strategies, and investing in in-house recruitment is an important result of this trend. Those companies that continue to use agencies are operating in a cash-strapped environment, and have succeeding in driving down agency costs significantly.

Now, recruitment agency margins are lower than ever and they are forced to rely on repeat business for survival. The client is king in this market, and relationships with candidates – once considered important to nurture – are now two-a-penny. Determined to remain competitive despite a difficult economic situation, business is demanding more and more accountability from recruitment agencies forcing them to prove their value over time. Those that can demonstrate this value survive. The others, those that offer short-term, quick-fix and often inappropriate solutions, disappear without a trace.

Don't call us, we'll call you (disruptive technological progress and an employer-driven market)

The economy may not be booming but technology entrepreneurs certainly aren't worried. The low-cost nature of their business means that they remain relatively unaffected by the change.

Web 2.0 was just the beginning. Now, technology in recruitment is so developed that HR numbers have fallen dramatically. Some believe that within a decade the HR industry will have disappeared. Powerful search engines and the shift in people's lives online allow employers to vet personalities before considering people for a job. Work, life, relationships – all of it has moved online, giving employers far more than a CV to judge their candidates on. Now, people laugh that their biggest privacy concern was once the doomed government ID cards scheme.

Rateyouremployee.com is feared by all. This site, developed in 2008, sorts the winners from the losers and has the power to make or break careers. Employers snigger at the thought that Vault was once an influential information source. It's still there, somewhere in the depths of the internet, but few employees bother to rate their employer – gratitude for having work and fear of being caught are adequate disincentives.

Employees and trade unions have tried to fight back, still banging the drum about employee rights, but employers reign all powerful, and really don't need to listen to anyone else. Some say the days of trade unions are numbered, already their influence has waned considerably and younger employees, so accustomed to the 'way things are', struggle to understand what they were once for.

Recruitment companies were initially slow to react to new technologies. The ones that survived embraced it and employed internet entrepreneurs to help them integrate technology into their business model. Now, IT graduates dominate in recruitment, as finding new ways to use the web and advising business about online recruitment have become core recruitment practices. Traditional recruiters work more closely with business, performing a whole new set of functions including HR consultancy and employee management.

Notes

1   A Smith, *The Wealth of Nations* (London, Oxford University Press, 1998).
2   For an account of how markets have become more complex over time see ED Beinhocker, *The Origin of Wealth: Evolution, complexity and the radical remaking of economics* (London: Random House, 2006).
3   SkillSoft survey material reported in *Recruiter Magazine*, available at www.recruitermagazine.co.uk/Articles/331931/60%20of%20employees%20see k%20new%20role.html (accessed 19 Mar 2007).
4   Chartered Institute of Personnel and Development (CIPD), *Recruitment, Retention and Turnover*, 2006 survey, available at www.cipd.co.uk/NR/rdonlyres/A5316993-E9EB-413D-A673-D1D6A5063DD3/0/recruitretntsurv06.pdf (accessed 9 Mar 2007).
5   'The battle for brainpower', *The Economist*, 7–13 Oct 2006.
6   Ibid.
7   'The war for talent', *Fast Company*, July 1998.
8   Learning and Skills Council, *National Employer Skills Survey* (London: LSC, 2006).
9   S Gillinson and D O'Leary, *Working Progress: How to reconnect young people and organisations* (London: Demos, 2006).
10 P Moss and C Tilly, *Soft Skills and Race: An investigation of black men's employment problems* (New York: Russell Sage Foundation, 1995).
11 CIPD, *Recruitment, Retention and Turnover*.
12 M White et al, *Managing to Change?* (Basingstoke: Palgrave, 2004).
13 Recruitment and Employment Confederation (REC) and Ernst and Young, *Annual Industry Turnover and Key Volumes Survey 2005/06*, available at www.rec.uk.com/rec/research/2006annualturnover.aspx (accessed 3 Apr 2007).
14 World Advertising Research Center, see www.warc.com/ (accessed 29 Mar 2007).
15 C Minto, *ONREC Conference and Exhibition, Report and Conclusions* (London, 2006).
16 Ibid.

17 REC Tracker trends, 2006, internal document.

18 comScore Jan 2007, see www.warc.com/ (accessed 29 Mar 2007).

19 REC Tracker trends, 2006.

20 'Cost of agency nurses "soars"', *BBC News Online*, 1 Nov 2004, available at http://news.bbc.co.uk/1/hi/health/3965117.stm (accessed 29 Mar 2007).

21 'Hewitt heckled by furious nurses', *BBC News Online*, 26 Apr 2006, available at http://news.bbc.co.uk/1/hi/health/4943596.stm (accessed 29 Mar 2007).

22 CIPD, 'Employee turnover and retention', factsheet, available at www.cipd.co.uk/subjects/hrpract/turnover/empturnretent.htm (accessed 21 Mar 2007).

23 World Bank ease of doing business indicators, 'Starting a business', see www.doingbusiness.org/ExploreTopics/StartingBusiness/Default.aspx?direction=asc&sort=2 (accessed 3 Apr 2007).

24 REC and Ernst and Young, *Annual Industry Turnover and Key Volumes Survey 2005/06*.

25 Cabinet Office, *Freedom and Fairness: The final report of the equalities review* (Norwich, HMSO, 2007).

26 CIPD, *Recruitment, Retention and Turnover*.

27 Smith, *Wealth of Nations*.

28 Equal Opportunities Commission, *Recruiting Staff: Guidance for managers and supervisors* (May 2006), available at www.eoc.org.uk/PDF/recruitment_and_selection_checklist.pdf (accessed 14 Mar 2007).

29 L Horner and A Jones, *Great Expectations: Understanding the motivations of migrant workers* (London: The Work Foundation, 2005).

30 Cabinet Office, *Freedom and Fairness*.

31 D Cameron, speech to Ethnic Media Conference, 29 Nov 2006.

32 Office of National Statistics, 2004.

33 J Huber and P Skidmore, *The New Old* (London: Demos, 2003).

34 UK Government Actuary Department (GAD), population projections, 2004.

35 Ibid.

36 Prime Minister's Strategy Unit, *Ethnic Minorities and the Labour Market* (London: Cabinet Office, 2003).

37 Economic and Social Research Council, *Women in the Workplace: The gender pay gap remains*, available at www.esrcsocietytoday.ac.uk/ESRCInfoCentre/PO/releases/2004/june/women.aspx?ComponentId=2069&SourcePageId=1405 (accessed 3 Apr 2007).

38 Office of National Statistics, www.statistics.gov.uk/cci/nugget.asp?id=1654 (accessed 3 Apr 2007).

39 H Green and S Parker, *The Other Glass Ceiling* (London: Demos, 2006).

40 Cabinet Office, *Freedom and Fairness*.

41 N Isles, *The Joy of Work* (London: The Work Foundation, 2004).

42 Ipsos MORI, Political Survey 2006, see www.ipsos-mori.com/polls/2006/st060813.shtml (accessed 7 Mar 2007).

43 P Legrain, *Immigrants: Your country needs them* (London: Little Brown, 2007).

44   See www.adecco.com/Channels/adeccoNewVI/aboutadecco/overview/
     overview1.asp (accessed 12 Mar 2007).

45   See www.tomorrowproject.net/pub/1__GLIMPSES/Individuals_and_identity/-
     202.html (accessed 12 March 2007).

46   Green and Parker, *Other Glass Ceiling*.

47   See www.natcen.ac.uk/natcen/pages/news_and_media_docs/BSA_
     %20press_release_jan07.pdf (accessed 3 Apr 2007).

48   Isles, *Joy of Work*.

49   'Masters of the universe', *The Economist*, 7–13 Oct 2006.

50   'Promotion more important than pay', *Recruiter Magazine*, 25 Oct 2006.

51   See www.cipd.co.uk/subjects/empreltns/psycntrct/psycontr.htm?IsSrchRes=1
     (accessed 3 Apr 2007).

52   J Chapman, *System Failure* (London: Demos, 2004).

53   StepStone International Online Recruitment, 'UK businesses fail to engage with
     staff', *Onrec.com*, 28 Nov 2006, see www.onrec.com/content2/
     archiveissue.asp?iid=84 (accessed 5 Apr 2007).

54   See http://europe.vault.com/companies/localesurveylists.jsp?country=
     United%20Kingdom&product_id=328&countVar=count (accessed 8 Mar
     2007).

55   Business in the Community, 'Engaging employees', see www.bitc.org.uk/
     events/ap_on_employees.html (accessed 29 Mar 2007).

56   Manpower, *What Makes a Great Employer?* (2005), available at
     www.manpower.se/Uploaded/FA0B4C69EDCF45E29CE79D6465FBB29F.pdf
     (accessed 8 Mar 2007).

57   R Cowe and S Williams, *Where are the Ethical Consumers?* (London: The Co-
     operative Bank, 2000).

58   S Gillinson and D O'Leary, *Working Progress: How to reconnect organisations
     and young people* (London: Demos, 2006).

59   City & Guilds, *Portfolio Careers* (London: City & Guilds, 2004).

60   R Taylor, *Britain's World of Work: Myths and realities* (Swindon, Economic and
     Social Research Council, 2002), see
     www.leeds.ac.uk/esrcfutureofwork/downloads/fow_publication_3.pdf
     (accessed 3 Apr 2007).

61   CIPD, *Recruitment, Retention and Turnover*.

62   *Leitch Review of Skills*, final report (London: HM Treasury, 2006), available at:
     www.hm-treasury.gov.uk/independent_reviews/leitch_review/
     review_leitch_index.cfm (accessed 3 Apr 2007).

63   Isles, *Joy of Work*.

64   CIPD, *Flexible Working: Impact and implementation* (London: CIPD, 2005).

65   L Grossman, 'Time's person of the year: You', *Time*, www.time.com/time/
     magazine/article/0,9171,1569514,00.html (accessed 8 Mar 2007).

66   'MySpace plans Japanese network', *Times Online*, 7 Nov 2006, available at
     http://business.timesonline.co.uk/tol/business/markets/japan/article627543.ece
     (accessed 4 Apr 2007).

67   E Mills, 'Is Google worth its weight in gold?', *CNET News.com*, 17 Nov 2006, see

http://news.com.com/Is+Google+worth+its+weight+in+gold/2100-1030_3-6136393.html (accessed 4 Apr 2007).

68 See http://pages.ebay.co.uk/aboutebay/thecompany/companyoverview.html (accessed 15 Mar 2007).

69 See www.simplyhired.com/aboutus.html (accessed 8 Mar 2007).

70 See www.linkedin.com/ (accessed 4 Apr 2007).

71 See www.zubka.com/ (accessed 4 Apr 2007).

72 See www.hpa.org.uk/radiation/publications/documents_of_nrpb/pdfs/doc_15_5.pdf (accessed 22 Mar 2007).

73 Recruiting in Cyberspace, LSE/ONREC conference 17 Jun 2004.

74 C Anderson, 'The long tail', *Wired Magazine* www.wired.com/wired/archive/12.10/tail_pr.html (accessed 29 Mar 2007).

75 R Axelrod, *The Evolution of Co-operation* (New York: Basic Books, 1984).

76 'How to keep the oil flowing in a dangerous world', Rupert Steiner interview with Lord Browne, *The Spectator*, 13 May 2006, available at www.spectator.co.uk/archive/business/21973/part_3/how-to-keep-the-oil-flowing-in-a-dangerous-world.thtml (accessed 29 Mar 2007).

77 See www.adamsmith.org/blog (accessed 4 Apr 2007).

78 http://blog.auctionbytes.com/cgi-bin/blog/blog.pl?/pl/2007/2/1171941688.html (accessed 29 Mar 2007).

79 Taskforce on Race Equality and Diversity in the Private Sector, *Race Equality: The benefits for responsible business* (London: ippr, 2004).

80 See www.stonewall.org.uk/workplace/32.asp#Business_case (accessed 3 Mar 2007).

81 REC and Ernst and Young, *Annual Industry Turnover and Key Volumes Survey 2005/06.*

82 Taskforce on Race Equality and Diversity in the Private Sector, *Race Equality.*

83 O Khan, *Why Preferential Policies can be Fair: Achieving equality for members of disadvantaged groups* (London: Runnymede Trust, 2006).

84 Prime Minister's Strategy Unit, *Ethnic Minorities and the Labour Market* (Cabinet Office, 2003).

85 Equalities Review, interim report, see www.theequalitiesreview.org.uk/upload/assets/www.theequalitiesreview.org.uk/interim_report.pdf (accessed 29 Mar 2007).

86 For further information on sector skills councils see www.ssda.org.uk (accessed 4 Apr 2007).

87 See www.ssda.org.uk/ssda/default.aspx?page=2 (accessed 20 Mar 2007).

88 'Expect recruiters to Google you for "digital dirt"', *Seattle Times*, 4 Sep 2005, available at http://seattletimes.nwsource.com/html/businesstechnology/2002470098_digitaldirt04.html (accessed 29 March 2007).

89 'MySpace is public space when it comes to job search', *Onrec.com*, 27 Jul 2007, available at www.onrec.com/content2/news.asp?ID=12761 (accessed 29 Mar 2007).

90 EJ Evans, *Thatcher and Thatcherism* (London: Routledge, 2005).

DEMOS – Licence to Publish

THE WORK (AS DEFINED BELOW) IS PROVIDED UNDER THE TERMS OF THIS LICENCE ("LICENCE"). THE WORK IS PROTECTED BY COPYRIGHT AND/OR OTHER APPLICABLE LAW. ANY USE OF THE WORK OTHER THAN AS AUTHORIZED UNDER THIS LICENCE IS PROHIBITED. BY EXERCISING ANY RIGHTS TO THE WORK PROVIDED HERE, YOU ACCEPT AND AGREE TO BE BOUND BY THE TERMS OF THIS LICENCE. DEMOS GRANTS YOU THE RIGHTS CONTAINED HERE IN CONSIDERATION OF YOUR ACCEPTANCE OF SUCH TERMS AND CONDITIONS.

1. **Definitions**
   a **"Collective Work"** means a work, such as a periodical issue, anthology or encyclopedia, in which the Work in its entirety in unmodified form, along with a number of other contributions, constituting separate and independent works in themselves, are assembled into a collective whole. A work that constitutes a Collective Work will not be considered a Derivative Work (as defined below) for the purposes of this Licence.
   b **"Derivative Work"** means a work based upon the Work or upon the Work and other pre-existing works, such as a musical arrangement, dramatization, fictionalization, motion picture version, sound recording, art reproduction, abridgment, condensation, or any other form in which the Work may be recast, transformed, or adapted, except that a work that constitutes a Collective Work or a translation from English into another language will not be considered a Derivative Work for the purpose of this Licence.
   c **"Licensor"** means the individual or entity that offers the Work under the terms of this Licence.
   d **"Original Author"** means the individual or entity who created the Work.
   e **"Work"** means the copyrightable work of authorship offered under the terms of this Licence.
   f **"You"** means an individual or entity exercising rights under this Licence who has not previously violated the terms of this Licence with respect to the Work, or who has received express permission from DEMOS to exercise rights under this Licence despite a previous violation.
2. **Fair Use Rights.** Nothing in this licence is intended to reduce, limit, or restrict any rights arising from fair use, first sale or other limitations on the exclusive rights of the copyright owner under copyright law or other applicable laws.
3. **Licence Grant.** Subject to the terms and conditions of this Licence, Licensor hereby grants You a worldwide, royalty-free, non-exclusive, perpetual (for the duration of the applicable copyright) licence to exercise the rights in the Work as stated below:
   a to reproduce the Work, to incorporate the Work into one or more Collective Works, and to reproduce the Work as incorporated in the Collective Works;
   b to distribute copies or phonorecords of, display publicly, perform publicly, and perform publicly by means of a digital audio transmission the Work including as incorporated in Collective Works;
   The above rights may be exercised in all media and formats whether now known or hereafter devised. The above rights include the right to make such modifications as are technically necessary to exercise the rights in other media and formats. All rights not expressly granted by Licensor are hereby reserved.
4. **Restrictions.** The licence granted in Section 3 above is expressly made subject to and limited by the following restrictions:
   a You may distribute, publicly display, publicly perform, or publicly digitally perform the Work only under the terms of this Licence, and You must include a copy of, or the Uniform Resource Identifier for, this Licence with every copy or phonorecord of the Work You distribute, publicly display, publicly perform, or publicly digitally perform. You may not offer or impose any terms on the Work that alter or restrict the terms of this Licence or the recipients' exercise of the rights granted hereunder. You may not sublicence the Work. You must keep intact all notices that refer to this Licence and to the disclaimer of warranties. You may not distribute, publicly display, publicly perform, or publicly digitally perform the Work with any technological measures that control access or use of the Work in a manner inconsistent with the terms of this Licence Agreement. The above applies to the Work as incorporated in a Collective Work, but this does not require the Collective Work apart from the Work itself to be made subject to the terms of this Licence. If You create a Collective Work, upon notice from any Licencor You must, to the extent practicable, remove from the Collective Work any reference to such Licensor or the Original Author, as requested.
   b You may not exercise any of the rights granted to You in Section 3 above in any manner that is primarily intended for or directed toward commercial advantage or private monetary

compensation. The exchange of the Work for other copyrighted works by means of digital file-sharing or otherwise shall not be considered to be intended for or directed toward commercial advantage or private monetary compensation, provided there is no payment of any monetary compensation in connection with the exchange of copyrighted works.

c If you distribute, publicly display, publicly perform, or publicly digitally perform the Work or any Collective Works, You must keep intact all copyright notices for the Work and give the Original Author credit reasonable to the medium or means You are utilizing by conveying the name (or pseudonym if applicable) of the Original Author if supplied; the title of the Work if supplied. Such credit may be implemented in any reasonable manner; provided, however, that in the case of a Collective Work, at a minimum such credit will appear where any other comparable authorship credit appears and in a manner at least as prominent as such other comparable authorship credit.

5. Representations, Warranties and Disclaimer

a By offering the Work for public release under this Licence, Licensor represents and warrants that, to the best of Licensor's knowledge after reasonable inquiry:

    i Licensor has secured all rights in the Work necessary to grant the licence rights hereunder and to permit the lawful exercise of the rights granted hereunder without You having any obligation to pay any royalties, compulsory licence fees, residuals or any other payments;

    ii The Work does not infringe the copyright, trademark, publicity rights, common law rights or any other right of any third party or constitute defamation, invasion of privacy or other tortious injury to any third party.

b EXCEPT AS EXPRESSLY STATED IN THIS LICENCE OR OTHERWISE AGREED IN WRITING OR REQUIRED BY APPLICABLE LAW, THE WORK IS LICENCED ON AN "AS IS" BASIS, WITHOUT WARRANTIES OF ANY KIND, EITHER EXPRESS OR IMPLIED INCLUDING, WITHOUT LIMITATION, ANY WARRANTIES REGARDING THE CONTENTS OR ACCURACY OF THE WORK.

6. Limitation on Liability. EXCEPT TO THE EXTENT REQUIRED BY APPLICABLE LAW, AND EXCEPT FOR DAMAGES ARISING FROM LIABILITY TO A THIRD PARTY RESULTING FROM BREACH OF THE WARRANTIES IN SECTION 5, IN NO EVENT WILL LICENSOR BE LIABLE TO YOU ON ANY LEGAL THEORY FOR ANY SPECIAL, INCIDENTAL, CONSEQUENTIAL, PUNITIVE OR EXEMPLARY DAMAGES ARISING OUT OF THIS LICENCE OR THE USE OF THE WORK, EVEN IF LICENSOR HAS BEEN ADVISED OF THE POSSIBILITY OF SUCH DAMAGES.

7. Termination

a This Licence and the rights granted hereunder will terminate automatically upon any breach by You of the terms of this Licence. Individuals or entities who have received Collective Works from You under this Licence, however, will not have their licences terminated provided such individuals or entities remain in full compliance with those licences. Sections 1, 2, 5, 6, 7, and 8 will survive any termination of this Licence.

b Subject to the above terms and conditions, the licence granted here is perpetual (for the duration of the applicable copyright in the Work). Notwithstanding the above, Licensor reserves the right to release the Work under different licence terms or to stop distributing the Work at any time; provided, however that any such election will not serve to withdraw this Licence (or any other licence that has been, or is required to be, granted under the terms of this Licence), and this Licence will continue in full force and effect unless terminated as stated above.

8. Miscellaneous

a Each time You distribute or publicly digitally perform the Work or a Collective Work, DEMOS offers to the recipient a licence to the Work on the same terms and conditions as the licence granted to You under this Licence.

b If any provision of this Licence is invalid or unenforceable under applicable law, it shall not affect the validity or enforceability of the remainder of the terms of this Licence, and without further action by the parties to this agreement, such provision shall be reformed to the minimum extent necessary to make such provision valid and enforceable.

c No term or provision of this Licence shall be deemed waived and no breach consented to unless such waiver or consent shall be in writing and signed by the party to be charged with such waiver or consent.

d This Licence constitutes the entire agreement between the parties with respect to the Work licensed here. There are no understandings, agreements or representations with respect to the Work not specified here. Licensor shall not be bound by any additional provisions that may appear in any communication from You. This Licence may not be modified without the mutual written agreement of DEMOS and You.